A GUIDE TO UK MONETARY POLICY

A GUIDE TO UK MONETARY POLICY

by

PAUL TEMPERTON

Palgrave Macmillan

ISBN 978-1-349-07998-8 ISBN 978-1-349-07996-4 (eBook)
DOI 10.1007/978-1-349-07996-4

Softcover reprint of the hardcover 1st edition 1986

Scholarly & Reference Division,
St. Martin's Press, Inc., 175 Fifth Avenue, New York, NY 10010

First published in the United States of America in 1986

ISBN 978-0-312-35306-3

Library of Congress Cataloging-in-Publication Data
Temperton, Paul, 1958–
A guide to UK monetary policy.
Includes index.
1. Monetary policy—Great Britain. 2. Interest rates—Great Britain. 3. Money market—Great Britain.
I. Title.
HG939.5.T45 1986 332.4'941 85–27867
ISBN 978-0-312-35306-3

To Nicky

Contents

List of Tables

List of Figures

Preface

The book was started in the Autumn of 1984 and finished a year later. Its central aim is to explain the way in which the UK authorities analyse monetary developments and implement monetary policy in the mid 1980s. The background to the introduction of monetary targets in the UK is discussed briefly in Chapter 1. The second chapter follows on with a discussion of the development of policy since the introduction of announced quantitative targets for monetary aggregates: in particular, the development of the Medium Term Financial Strategy is examined. Chapters 3 and 4 concentrate on the analysis of broad and narrow money, respectively. Chapter 3 is based on a paper produced by the author for Hoare Govett in 1984; that paper was, in turn, a revised version of a Hoare Govett paper written by Tony Hotson in 1980. As well as the behaviour of the targetted monetary aggregates, various other indicators are examined by the UK monetary authorities (defined as the Bank of England,the Treasury and the Ministers responsible for economic policy) when coming to a judgement about the stance of policy. In particular, the behaviour of the exchange rate has been a most influential factor during the 1980s. Chapter 5 attempts to explain the various factors which are taken into account by the authorities, when coming to a decision about the stance of policy and the appropriate level of short term interest rates. Short term control of broad money in the UK has come to rely to a large extent on the authorities' funding behaviour and this is discussed in Chapters 7 and 8.

While the aim of the book is to provide a guide to the way in which the authorities analyse monetary developments and conduct monetary policy it must be recognised that there exists a wide diversity of opinion on such matters. The final chapter, therefore, attempts to draw attention to some of the more important continuing questions surrounding monetary policy in the UK: it may be read on its own as a general overview.

A large number of people have helped with the production of the book. Hoare Govett provided many of the facilities used in its production, in particular those for typesetting and the drawing of charts. Theresa Willson carried out the typesetting with efficiency and speed and was thus of central importance in the book's production. Samantha Lear prepared the charts. Many people commented on the draft version of the book: Barry Johnston, Tony Hotson, David Porter and David Willetts should be singled out for special thanks in this respect. I remain, of course, responsible for any errors which remain.

Paul Temperton October 1985.

List of Abbreviations

(publications are shown in italic)

Bank	Bank of England
BB	Bankers' operational balances held with the Bank of England
BEQB	*Bank of England Quarterly Bulletin*
CCC	Competition and Credit Control
CD	Certificate of Deposit
CG	Central Government
CGBR	Central Government Borrowing Requirement
CGD	Sales of central government debt to the banks, non-bank private sector and overseas net of Bank of England purchases of bills
CRD	Cash ratio deposits held by banks at the Bank of England
DCE	Domestic Credit Expansion
EEA	Exchange Equalisation Account
ELs	Eligible liabilities
FS	*Financial Statistics*, published monthly by HMSO
FSBR	*Financial Statement and Budget Report*, otherwise known as the 'Red Book', which is published each year on the day of the Budget
HMT	Her Majesty's Treasury
IBELs	Interest Bearing Eligible Liabilities
IDCB	Issue Department holdings of commercial bills
IMF	International Monetary Fund
LAs	Local Authorities
LABR	Local Authorities' Borrowing Requirement
LCB	London Clearing Bank
LDMA	London Discount Market Association
LDT	Licensed deposit-taker
LIBOR	London Interbank Offered Rate
MLR	Minimum Lending Rate
MTFS	Medium Term Financial Strategy
NAC	Notes and coin held by both the bank and non-bank private sectors

NNDL	Net Non-Deposit Liabilities
NNDL$	Foreign currency NNDL
NNDL£	Sterling NNDL
NSB	National Savings Bank
OF$	Official foreign currency borrowing
OPS	Other public sector
OS£D	Overseas sector deposits in sterling with UK monetary sector
OS$D	Overseas sector deposits in foreign currencies with UK monetary sector
OS£L	Lending by UK monetary sector in sterling to overseas sector
OS$L	Lending by UK monetary sector in foreign currencies to overseas sector
OS£G	Sales of UK public sector debt to overseas sector
PCs	Public Corporations
PCBR	Public Corporations' borrowing requirement
PRV£D	UK private sector deposits in sterling with UK monetary sector
PRV$D	UK private sector deposits in foreign currencies with UK monetary sector
PRV£L	Lending by UK monetary sector in sterling to UK private sector
PRV$L	Lending by UK monetary sector in foreign currencies to UK private sector
PRV£G	Sales of public sector debt to UK non-bank private sector
PRVNAC	UK non-bank private sector holdings of notes and coin
PSBR	Public Sector Borrowing Requirement
PUB£D	UK public sector deposits in sterling with UK monetary sector
PUB£L	Lending by UK monetary sector in sterling to public sector
PUB$D	UK public sector deposits in foreign currencies with UK monetary sector
PUB$L	Lending by UK monetary sector in foreign currencies to public sector
REPO	Sale and repurchase agreement
RES	International Reserves in the EEA
RPI	UK Retail Prices Index
SCB	Scottish Clearing Bank
SSD	Supplementary Special Deposits

Glossary of Terms

Accepting House: Traditionally accepting houses specialised in accepting (or guaranteeing) bills; they now have a wider banking role. There are sixteen accepting houses in London represented on the Accepting Houses Committee. The members are N.M. Rothschild & Sons Ltd.; Baring Bros. & Co. Ltd.; Brown Shipley & Co. Ltd.; Charterhouse Japhet plc.; Robert Fleming & Co. Ltd.; Guinness Mahon & Co. Ltd.; Hambros Bank Ltd.; Hill Samuel & Co. Ltd.; Kleinwort Benson Ltd.; Lazard Bros. & Co. Ltd.; Samuel Montagu & Co. Ltd.; Morgan Grenfell & Co. Ltd.; Rea Bros plc.; J. Henry Schroder Wagg & Co. Ltd.; Singer & Friedlander Ltd.; and S.G. Warburg & Co. Ltd.

Asset Management: The process whereby banks adjust the volume of their loans to equal the supply of deposits (the opposite process is termed *liability management*).

Bank Return: A weekly return from the Bank (released at 3 p.m. each Thursday) giving the balance sheets of the Bank's Issue and Banking Departments.

Banking Month: Defined as the period between monthly *make-up days.*

Banking Sector: The banking sector was replaced by the *monetary sector* at the end of 1981. It comprised those institutions included on the statistical lists of banks and discount market institutions, together with the Banking Department of the Bank of England. Inclusion on the statistical lists was based on informal appraisal of a bank's size and reputation and was usually closely linked with the granting of authorised bank status for exchange control purposes.

Banking Statistics: A monthly press release from the Bank giving new and revised data on some of the tables in the *BEQB.*

Base Drift: If a new *monetary target* has a base level which is higher than the mid point of the previous target, base drift is said to occur.

Bill Arbitrage: Alternatively referred to as bill *round tripping*, see below. Hard arbitrage refers to the practice of borrowing on bills in order to place the funds on deposit (at the same maturity) at a profitable margin. Such arbitrage inflates both bank lending to the private sector and *£M3*. Soft arbitrage involves switching to bill finance from other forms of finance (e.g. a base rate related overdraft); it does not inflate bank lending and *£M3*.

Bill Leak: The level of bills held by the non-bank private sector.

Bill Mountain: The portfolio of commercial bills held by the Bank of England. As the amount of intervention by the Bank in the money market has increased in recent years, the quantity of bills held by the Bank has increased substantially, standing at around £15bn in mid-1985.

Broad Money: Broad money refers to money held as a form of savings as well as money held for transactions purposes. It provides a measure of the private sector's holdings of relatively liquid assets — i.e. those which could be converted with relative ease and without capital loss into spending on goods and services.

Bulldog Bonds: Bonds issued by overseas institutions and denominated in sterling.

Cash Ratio Deposits: These are non-interest bearing deposits which all institutions in the UK *monetary sector* must keep with the Bank. They are essentially a tax on the members of the monetary sector and are designed to provide income and resources for the Bank. They do not form any part of a system of *monetary base control.* The level is adjusted twice a year, normally on the third Monday after the April and October *make-up days*, and is at the rate of ½% of *eligible liabilities.*

Contingent Liability: A liability which is contingent on some other event. For example, a bank underwriting a bill will only have the liability to pay should the original drawer of the bill default.

Corset: See *SSD.*

Covered Interest Rate Differential: The differential between interest rates on instruments in different currencies after allowing for forward cover in the foreign exchange market. See *Forward Exchange Market*.

Discount Houses (& LDMA): The group of institutions whose traditional activity is the discounting of bills issued either by companies or the Treasury. The nine discount houses forming the London Discount Market Association (LDMA) are: Alexanders Discount; Cater Allen; Clive Discount; Gerrard and National; King and Shaxson; Quin Cope; Seccombe, Marshall and Campion; Smith St. Aubyn; and Union Discount.

Discount Window: The term used to describe the mechanism through which the Bank lends to the money market in order to relieve shortages of cash.

Disintermediation: The process whereby business which was previously intermediated by the banking system becomes channelled through other institutions. 'Cosmetic' disintermediation occurs if the bank still acts as an intermediary but the business does not appear on its balance sheet.

Domestic Credit Expansion: Domestic Credit Expansion is equivalent to the sum of the domestic counterparts to *£M3* growth plus bank lending in sterling to overseas.

Eligible Liabilities: The eligible liabilities of the UK *monetary sector* comprise basically their sterling *sight* and *time deposits* net of balances held with certain approved institutions. Specifically, eligible liabilities comprise: sight deposits (except those of overseas offices); time deposits, other than those of overseas offices, with an original maturity of two years or less; CDs issued; promissory notes, bills and other short term paper issued; items in suspense; 60% of credit items in the course of transmission; and net sterling liabilities to overseas offices (an overall net claim not being treated as an offset). From this total is subtracted the sum of: 60% of debit items in the course of collection; balances with the Bank (excluding *special deposits* and *cash ratio deposits*); secured and unsecured money with the *LDMA*; and secured money at call with money brokers and gilt edged jobbers.

Equity Withdrawal: A term normally used in relation to the housing market. It is said to occur if net new loans for house purchase exceed net private sector expenditure on housing.

Eurocurrency Deposits: Deposits with a bank that is not located in the country in whose currency the deposit is denominated. For example, dollars deposited in a London bank are called eurodollars; sterling deposited in a New York bank is called eurosterling.

Forward Exchange Market: A market in which contracts are made to supply currencies at fixed dates in the future at fixed prices.

Funding: The term originally applied to the process of converting short term to long term debt. Government funding thus involved issuing longer dated instruments (e.g. *gilt edged stocks*) to replace *Treasury bills*. More recently the term has been used to refer to the total amount of government debt (both short and long term as well as National Savings) sold to the non-bank private sector.

Gilt edged stocks (Gilts): Stocks, issued by the government, normally paying a fixed amount of interest (in the form of a 'coupon') per year and having an *original maturity* of several years.

Intermediation: The process whereby funds are channelled, via an intermediary, from one sector of the economy to another. For example, banks may act as intermediaries between the personal sector (traditionally a net saver) and the company sector (traditionally a net borrower).

Liability Management: The process whereby banks adjust the volume of their deposits in order to accommodate changes in the demand for loans (the opposite process is termed *asset management).*

'Lifeboat': The term used to refer to the joint operation by the Bank and the clearing banks in 1973 to support the 'secondary' banks.

M0: M0 is a measure of *narrow money*, and is alternatively termed the wide *monetary base* as it includes all the possible components of a monetary base measure. These are notes and coin held by the non-bank private sector, banks' holdings of cash (*till money*) and bankers' operational balances at the Bank of England. M0 is currently the authorities' targetted measure of *narrow money.*

M1: A narrow measure of money comprising notes and coin in circulation with the public and the private sector's sterling *sight deposits*. Sterling *sight deposits* can be classified as either interest bearing or non-interest bearing. Adding just the non-interest bearing deposits to notes and coin gives the measure non-interest bearing M1 (or nib M1).

M2: A specially devised measure of transactions balances which comprises non-interest bearing M1, private sector interest bearing retail sterling bank deposits, private sector holdings of retail building society deposits and NSB ordinary accounts.

M3: M3, alternatively referred to as Total M3, is a measure of broad money. It adds to *sterling M3* UK private sector foreign currency bank deposits.

Make-up Day: The day on which the banks make up their balance sheets for submission to the Bank. For the monthly banking statistics, make-up day is on the third Wednesday of each month (apart from December when it is the second Wednesday).

Monetary Base: The monetary base is defined as a subset of the monetary liabilities of the Bank of England. The three components which may be included are: (i) notes and coin in circulation with the public; (ii) notes and coin held by banks (as *till money*); and (iii) bankers' *operational deposits* at the Bank of England. *M0*, the wide measure of the monetary base, includes all three components.

Monetary Base Control: A method of monetary control which relies on the authorities influencing the level of *monetary base*.

Monetary Sector: The UK monetary sector comprises: (a) all recognised banks and LDTs; (b) the National Girobank; (c) the trustee savings banks; (d) the Banking Department of the Bank of England; and (e) those banks in the Channel Islands and the Isle of Man which have chosen to comply with the current monetary control arrangements. The monetary sector replaced the *banking sector* at the end of 1981. Broadly it differs from the banking sector in that it includes all recognised banks and LDTs (rather than just those on the statistical list), the trustee savings banks and the National Girobank.

Monetary Target: A target, normally expressed as a range (say, 5-9%), for the growth of one or more measures of the money supply.

Narrow Money: Narrow money refers to money balances which are readily available to finance current spending, i.e. for 'transactions purposes'.

Off Balance Sheet Business: Banking business which is effectively carried out by a bank but which is not recorded on its balance sheet. For example, a bank may underwrite a bill which is then sold to the non-bank private sector. The bank is effectively acting as an intermediary but the business does not appear on its balance sheet.

Operational Deposits: These are deposits of the LCBs held at the Bank which are used for settling transactions between themselves and the Bank.

Original Maturity: The original maturity of an instrument is the term to maturity when the bill is issued.

Overfunding: The process whereby the Bank sells more government debt to the non-bank private sector than is needed to finance (or 'fund') the PSBR.

Private Sector Liquidity (PSL): Measures of private sector liquidity are normally distinguished from measures of money. They include selected liquid assets of the private sector whereas the monetary aggregates comprise selected components of the monetary sector's balance sheet (plus notes and coin in circulation with the public). The two most widely used PSL measures are *PSL1* and *PSL2.*

PSL1: PSL1 is a measure of *Private Sector Liquidity*. It includes all the components of *£M3* (apart from private sector sterling *time deposits* with an *original maturity* of over two years) as well as private sector holdings of money market instruments (bank bills, *Treasury bills*, local authority deposits) and certificates of tax deposit.

PSL2: PSL2 adds to *PSL1* private sector holdings of building society deposits (excluding term shares and SAYE) and National Savings instruments (excluding certificates, SAYE and other longer-term deposits) but, to avoid double-counting, excludes building society holdings of money market instruments and bank deposits.

Reserve Assets Ratio: Between September 1971 and August 1981, banks were required to keep a certain proportion of their *eligible liabilities* as reserve assets. The ratio was 12½% for the period up to January 1981, when it was reduced to 10%. It was temporarily reduced to 8% for most of March and April 1981 and abolished in August 1981. Reserve assets comprised:

i) Balances at the Bank (other than special deposits or *supplementary special deposits*)
ii) British Government and Northern Ireland *Treasury bills*

iii) Secured money at call with the London discount market
iv) British government stocks with a *residual maturity* of less than one year
v) Local authority bills eligible for rediscount at the Bank
vi) Commercial bills eligible for rediscount at the Bank, up to a maximum of 2% of *eligible liabilities*.

Residual Maturity: The remaining term to maturity of an instrument. For example, a bill with an *original maturity* of three months issued two months ago has a residual maturity of one month.

Round-Tripping: The process whereby funds raised in one market are deposited in another to yield a profit. For example, a company may issue a bill and deposit the proceeds in the money market to yield a higher return (this process is also referred to as *bill arbitrage*).

Sale and Repurchase Agreement (REPO): An agreement whereby instruments are sold with an agreement to repurchase them at a specified future date.

Seasonal Adjustment: The process whereby recurrent variations in a series of data are removed.

Sight Deposits: Deposits which are withdrawable without notice. Sight deposits which are non-interest bearing consist predominantly of current (chequable) accounts. Sight deposits which are interest bearing include both current accounts and money market deposits which are withdrawable on demand.

Special Deposits: The authorities can call on the banks to place a certain percentage of their *eligible liabilities* in a special deposit at the Bank which is non-interest bearing. They have not been called since 1980. These deposits did not count as reserve assets when the *reserve assets ratio* was in place.

Spot Exchange Market: The market in which currencies are traded for immediate delivery, as opposed to the *forward exchange market.*

Sterling M3 (£M3): £M3 is a measure of *broad money*. It comprises notes and coin held by the public plus all of the UK private sector's sterling deposits (both sight and time) held in UK banks. £M3 is currently the authorities' targetted measure of *broad money.*

Supplementary Special Deposits (SSD): The Supplementary Special Deposit Scheme was a scheme which imposed penalties on the banking system for expanding their interest bearing *eligible liabilities* at a rate faster than that prescribed by the Bank of England. The scheme operated in three periods: December 1973 to February 1975; November 1976 to August 1977, and June 1978 to June 1980.

Tender: An offer to buy at a fixed price. For example, the *discount houses* at the weekly *Treasury bill* tender will offer to take up so many bills at a certain price.

Term Structure: The relationship between interest rates (and/or yields) at different maturities. For bonds, this is often expressed as a *yield curve*.

Till Money: The quantity of notes and coin held by banks. Alternatively termed *vault cash*.

Time Deposits: Deposits for which notice has to be given before they can be withdrawn without penalty.

Total M3: See M3.

Town Clearing: The town clearing facility enables a cheque for more than £10,000 drawn on an office of a London Clearing Bank located within a specified area of the City, to be presented by any such other office at the town clearing for settlement on the same day. The settlement takes place after the banks have closed for business.

Treasury Bills: Short term bills (normally three months maturity) issued by the government.

Vault Cash: See *till money*.

Wholesale deposits: Large deposits bearing an interest rate in line with market rates: for example, CDs.

Yield Curve: A curve showing the relationship between yields on bonds at different maturities. It is one of the most popular ways of expressing the *term structure*.

1 Background to the Introduction of Monetary Targets in the UK

The movement towards the use of announced, quantitative targets for the growth of the money supply in the UK started in the mid-1960s. During the 1950s and early 1960s, the UK economy grew at a rate which was sufficient to keep unemployment at a very low level. Economic policy was aimed largely at 'managing demand' so as to achieve such a level of activity. The constraint on the government's demand management was the maintenance of the value of the exchange rate at $2.80 to the £. When economic growth became too rapid, and the balance of payments deteriorated, economic policy would become more restrictive in order to moderate demand, correct the balance of payments position and hence moderate pressure on the exchange rate. In the period of correction, any balance of payments deficit was met largely by running down the official foreign exchange reserves.

The policy of maintaining economic activity at (close to) the full employment level led to a steady increase in the public sector's involvement in the economy. The ratio of public expenditure to GDP rose, as shown in Figure 1.1, from 25% in 1955 to around 30% in the early 1970s. Inflation, in large part pulled by the continually high level of demand in the economy, also displayed a clear upward trend. Comparing the levels of inflation reached at comparable times in each of the business cycles since the mid 1950s, inflation rose steadily (Table 1.1).

Monetary policy in the 1960s was concerned primarily with the management of the level of nominal interest rates and the control of bank lending to the private sector. In turn, policy decisions were driven by the need to maintain the fixed exchange rate. From 1964 the authorities imposed quantitative ceilings on bank lending to the private sector. Within these ceilings, guidance was given about the sectors of the economy to which the available credit should be channelled: broadly, exporters and investors were favoured at the expense of the personal sector. Policy was not explicitly concerned with the growth of any measure of the money supply. Monetary data were collected from 1959[1] but the accepted view was that the relationship between the money supply and prices and incomes in the

Figure 1.1: Ratio of government expenditure to GDP, 1955 to 1985

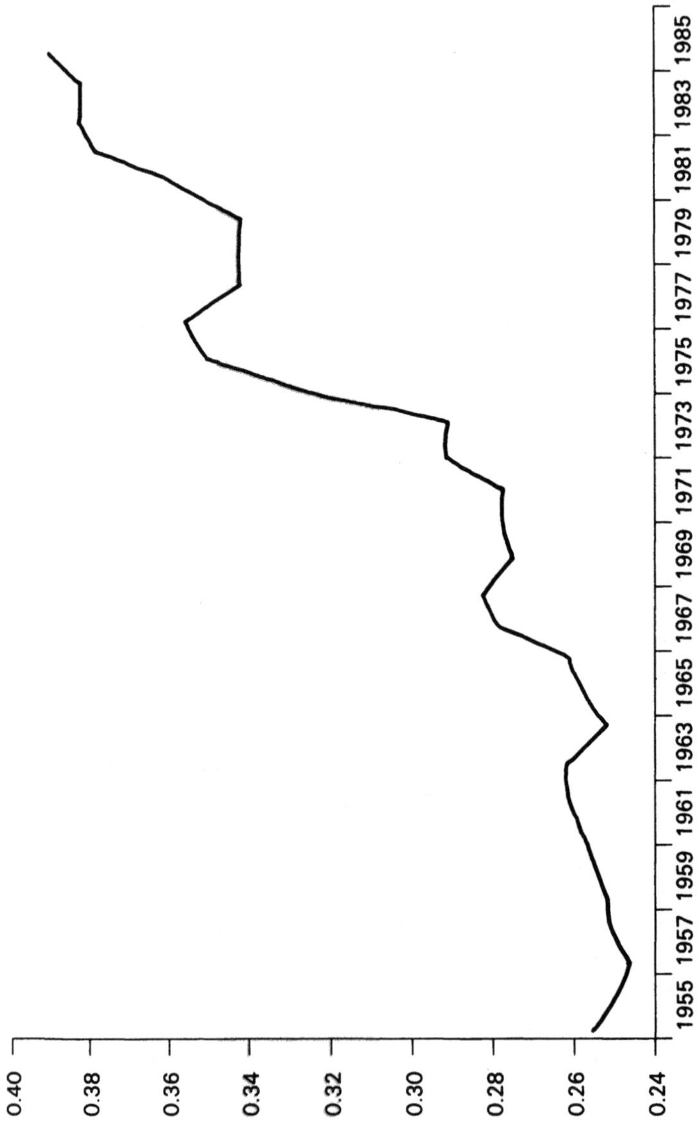

Ratio of central government total current expenditure to GDP at market prices.

Table 1.1: Inflation trends, 1958-1981*

Rate of Inflation:	**% p.a.:**
December 1958	1.9
January 1963	2.7
March 1967	3.5
February 1972	8.1
August 1975	26.9
May 1981	11.7

* the dates chosen are those corresponding to the troughs in each of the business cycles

economy was so unpredictable that it was highly unlikely to be a useful variable to examine for policy purposes.

Maintenance of the dollar/sterling exchange rate at $2.80 lasted from 1949 to 1967. In 1967, when a prolonged period of restrictive policies had failed to produce any correction of the balance of payments, the exchange rate was devalued from $2.80 to $2.40 and the UK obtained a loan from the IMF in order to bolster the foreign exchange reserves. The conditions attached to the loan obliged the UK to restrict the PSBR, restrain finance to the private sector and hence bring about more moderate Domestic Credit Expansion (DCE). The relationship between the PSBR, bank lending, government debt sales and DCE could be expressed within the new flow of funds accounting framework in a way which brought a greater coherence and consistency to the analysis of fiscal and monetary policies. As the size of the PSBR was constrained by the need to meet this restriction on DCE, the use of discretionary changes in the government's budgetary position to manage demand became even more restricted.

Although control of this credit measure was thus forced upon the UK by the IMF, two other key developments also led to greater attention being placed on money and credit. First, as inflation rose and became more volatile, the behaviour of nominal interest rates became a much less reliable guide to the stance of monetary policy. The expected real interest rate is equal to the nominal interest rate less the expected rate of inflation. In times of high and volatile inflation, inflationary expectations became much more difficult to assess. Hence, the authorities cannot know with any degree of certainty the prevailing real interest rate. Second, econometric work which had been carried out on the monetary data collected since 1959 came up with the conclusion that the demand for money could be satisfactorily explained by a few other economic variables: prices, incomes and interest rates. Moreover, the studies implied that control of the growth of the money supply could be achieved by acceptable variations in short term interest rates. Thus money could be controlled by changing interest rates; and direct controls may not be needed. At the time, there was a general movement towards favouring more competition in banking; given this background, and the evidence of the econometric studies, direct controls on lending were abandoned in September 1971.

At around the same time, the US authorities suspended the dollar's convertibility into gold, and the post-war system of fixed exchange rates was abandoned. After a short experiment in the 'snake' (the European fixed exchange rate system), the UK authorities decided to 'float' sterling on 23rd June 1972.

Shortly before that, the Conservative government had embarked on a highly expansionary fiscal policy (in the March 1972 Budget). The combination of such a stimulative fiscal policy and the new-found freedom of the banks to meet a strong demand for credit (financed by the increasingly popular liability management technique of bidding for deposits), produced a high level of demand in the economy and 'severe inflationary pressures ensued'[2]. Despite sharp rises in interest rates, rapid growth of money and credit persisted. Bank lending to the private sector grew by 33%, and M3 by 28%, in 1973. The econometric relationships based on the data of the 1960s (suggesting M3 could be brought under control by varying interest rates) had clearly 'broken down' in the face of the structural change in the banking system. Narrow measures of money, however, grew only modestly during the period. M1, for example, grew by only 5% (perhaps because money shifted from sight deposits to time deposits in response to the higher level of interest rates). Given the divergent movements of broad and narrow measures of money, interpretation of monetary conditions was not straightforward. With hindsight, however, the rapid growth of M3 in 1972 and 1973 was seen to be closely correlated with the behaviour of inflation in 1974 and 1975 (see Figure 1.2).

Even without that evidence, and in the face of the 'breakdown' of the econometric equations for M3, 'the course of M3 was a fairly strong policy constraint after 1973'[3]. Containment of M3, however, once again came to rely on a form of direct control on the banking system: the Supplementary Special Deposits Scheme (SSD or, more commonly, the 'corset') was introduced in December 1973 (see Chapter 3). M3's key attribute appeared to

Figure 1.2: Broad money and inflation, 1971 to 1985

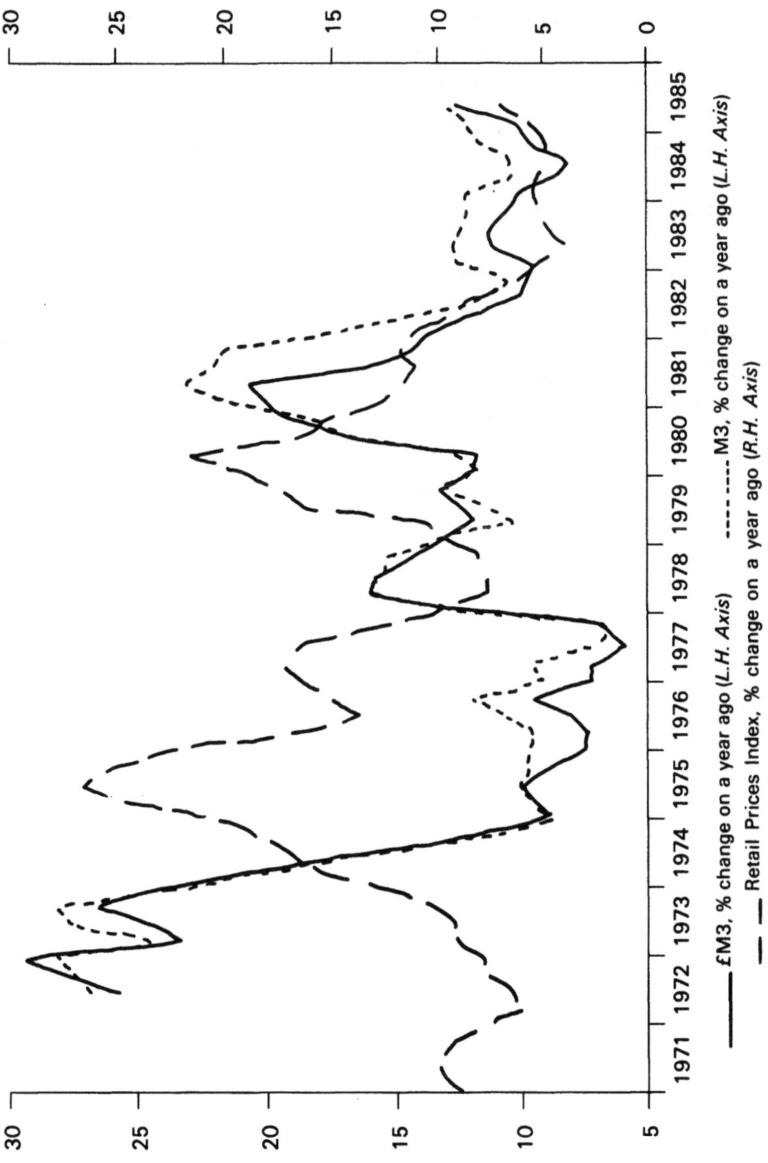

be the way in which it could be expressed in terms of its 'credit counterparts' — DCE (in turn reflecting the PSBR, the extent to which it was financed by debt sales to the non-bank private sector and bank lending to the private sector) and the influence of external flows. The counterparts framework has been the central feature of the analysis of UK monetary developments since that time.

Notes and References

1. Following the Report of the Radcliffe Committee: 'Report of the Committee on the Working of the Monetary System', Command 827, (London: HMSO, 1959).
2. J. S. Fforde, 'Setting Monetary Objectives', *BEQB*, June 1983, p.202.
3. J. S. Fforde, op cit., p.203.

2 Monetary Targets in the UK

(i) The introduction of monetary targets

The first monetary targets in the UK were set in the mid 1970s: these were informal, specifying guidelines and anticipated outturns for broad money growth and domestic credit. In the Budget of 6th April 1976, Denis Healey (Chancellor of the Exchequer) said that 'after two years in which M3 has grown a good deal more slowly than money GDP, I would expect their respective growth rates to come more into line in the coming financial year' (implying unchanged velocity, see below). Later on in the year, statements about the expected behaviour of the monetary aggregates became more definite. According to Fforde[1] 'the UK authorities had become caught in a spiral of declining confidence' in 1976. Exchange rate weakness, coupled with a continuing concern about the government's fiscal stance and the size of the PSBR, led to concern about the viability of the government's incomes policy (and, hence, future inflation).

In this environment, the government's funding programme was particularly difficult: this in turn led to problems with controlling M3. When it became clear that financial confidence would not be obtained without it, a published M3 target was announced. On 22nd July 1976 the Chancellor announced that the target rate of increase in M3 was to be 12% during the 1976/77 financial year. This was viewed as consistent with the likely £9bn DCE originally forecast in December 1975. In December 1976, in the 'letter of intent' to the IMF, the monetary objectives were again restated. Although DCE was still expected to be £9bn in 1976/77, the monetary expansion compatible with this was expressed in terms of Sterling M3 (£M3) (i.e. M3 minus UK residents' foreign currency deposits). For 1976/77 the growth of £M3 was expected to be 9%-13%. Targets for the growth of £M3 have been in place continuously since that time (see Table 2.1 and Figure 2.1).

External confidence improved markedly following the December measures; indeed, there was strong upward pressure on the exchange rate. Two methods were used to control the appreciation. First, heavy official sales of sterling were made in the foreign exchange market. Although

Table 2.1: Monetary targets set in the UK and results achieved

(£M3 unless otherwise stated)
(% growth at annual rate, seasonally adjusted)

		Target Set	Outturn	
1976/77 (fin. year)		9-13	8.0	
1977/78 (fin. year)		9-13	15.1	
1978/79 (fin. year)		8-12	11.4	(10.9 to October 78)[1]
October 78/October 79		8-12	13.7	(12.4 to June 79)[2]
June 79/October 80[3]		7-11	17.2	(9.9 to February 80)[4] (10.4 to April 80)
February 80/April 81		7-11	19.4	
February 81/April 82		6-10	12.8	
February 82/April 83:	M1	8-12	12.4	
	£M3	"	11.2	
	PSL2	"	11.6	
February 83/April 84:	M1	7-11	14.0	
	£M3	"	9.5	
	PSL2	"	12.6	
February 84/April 85:	MO	4-8	5.7	
	£M3	6-10	11.9	
1985/86	MO	3-7	-	
	£M3	5-9	-	

NOTES
[1] New target after six months.
[2] New target after eight months.
[3] Original target was to April 1980. Target was extended in October 1979 for one year.
[4] New target after eight months.

some of the increase in the foreign exchange reserves was used to repay loans taken out over the previous three years, the external flows still proved to be a highly expansionary influence on £M3 (for an explanation of this, see Chapter 3, section (v)). Second, interest rates were cut sharply. Minimum lending rate (MLR) fell from a peak level of 15% in October 1976 to 5% in October 1977 (see Appendix 1 for a list of the dates of MLR changes). Again, this was found to be undermining control of the domestic monetary aggregates:

> Until the end of October 1977 the pound was allowed to move against the dollar in such a way as to keep its effective exchange rate

> steady, and the index was held within the range 61.7 to 62.6; market purchases of sterling were heavy. On 31st October, official intervention to prevent a rise in the index was withdrawn because it was feared that such intervention would, if continued, prevent achievement of the authorities' monetary objectives[2].

The measures to control the appreciation of the exchange rate 'had collided with the overriding monetary constraint; and they were abandoned'[3].

The importance of the overriding monetary constraint was further demonstrated in the summer of 1978 when the government's fiscal policy was corrected and direct credit controls reintroduced once (market) confidence in the containment of £M3 growth became undermined. Control of inflation, however, still depended to a large degree on direct restraint of prices and incomes.

(ii) The development of the Medium Term Financial Strategy (MTFS)

After the election in May 1979 of the Conservative Government, economic and financial policy was changed radically. The measures taken in the first Conservative Budget, only six weeks after the election, fell into three broad groups. First, there was a major shift from direct to indirect taxation. The top marginal rate of tax on earned income was cut from 83% to 60%, and the basic rate from 33% to 30%. To help pay for this, the rate of VAT was raised from the split level of 8% and 12½% to one uniform level of 15%. Second, a wide range of controls were ended: pay, price and dividend controls were abolished; and a phased removal of exchange controls was announced. Indeed, only three months later (on 23rd September) it was announced that all remaining exchange controls were to be removed with effect from 24th October. Notably, however, the 'corset' was retained (see Chapter 3). These two groups of measures were designed to stimulate the 'supply side' of the economy by improving incentives to work and eliminating some of the bureaucratic obstacles to the efficient working of markets. Third, the money supply was moved to the centre of economic and financial strategy. The ultimate objective was to reduce inflation: control of the money supply was seen as the indispensable intermediate goal to achieving this final objective. £M3 was retained as the chosen measure of money. Its target growth rate was reduced from 8-12% to 7-11% for the period June 1979 to April 1980 (the target period was extended in October 1979 for one year). To reinforce the new government's counter-inflationary resolve, MLR was raised from 12% to 14%.

The MTFS made its appearance in the second Conservative Budget (26th March 1980). The government's objectives for the medium term were 'to bring down the rate of inflation and to create conditions for a sustainable growth of output and employment' (*FSBR*, 1980/81). The importance of the control of money was reaffirmed: 'control of the money supply will over a period of years reduce the rate of inflation' and an important change of emphasis was made. Plans for a progressive reduction in monetary growth over a number of years were made public. Thus, as Table 2.2 shows, the March 1980 Budget envisaged monetary growth declining from 7-11% in 1980/81 to 4-8% in 1983/84. Control of monetary growth was to be linked to control of the size of the PSBR in relation to GDP (the relationship between £M3 and its credit counterparts, discussed fully in Chapter 3, provided a framework within which the two were linked). The 1980 Budget envisaged that ratio falling from 3¾% in 1980/81 to 1½% in 1983/84 (see Table 2.3).

The MTFS was 'monetarist' in the sense that it was based on the quantity theory of money. This theory is founded on the identity that

$$MV = PT$$

where M is the stock of money and V its velocity of circulation (the number of times it changes hands in any particular period), P is the average price and T the total number of transactions in the economy. Thus the total amount of money spent in a particular time period must be identical to the value of transactions which it finances. If the velocity of circulation of money is reasonably stable and predictable, then there will be a close relationship between the growth of money and nominal expenditure in the economy. Traditionally, quantity theorists had thought that the output of the economy was also relatively fixed in the short run, thus leading to the conclusion that any rise in M would automatically raise P.

The MTFS made the assumption (more realistic in the 1980s) that with monetary growth set on a declining path, the course of output in the economy would depend on how quickly inflationary expectations were changed. The government was resigned to the fact that these would not change instantly and thought that 'the process of reducing inflation almost inevitably entails some loss of output initially' (*FSBR*, 1980/81). In the labour market, in particular, it was thought that with monetary growth restricted, excessively high wage demands would simply price people out of work. As a corollary, it was pointed out that 'the sooner inflation comes down, the faster the rate of economic growth that can be accommodated within the monetary guidelines' (*FSBR*, 1980/81).

The announcement of medium term monetary growth guidelines was, in itself, thought to be a key influence on inflationary expectations. The Green

Table 2.2: The MTFS and monetary growth

Targets/ projections set on:	Monetary Aggregate(s)	80/1	81/2	82/3	83/4	84/5	85/6	86/7	87/8	88/9
26 Mar 80	£M3	7-11	6-10	5-9	4-8					
10 Mar 81	£M3		6-10	5-9	4-8					
9 Mar 82	£M3, M1, PSL2			8-12	7-11	6-10				
15 Mar 83	£M3, M1, PSL2				7-11	6-10	5-9			
13 Mar 84	£M3					6-10	5-9	4-8	3-7	2-6
	MO					4-8	3-7	2-6	1-5	0-4
19 Mar 85	£M3						5-9	4-8	3-7	2-6
	MO						3-7	2-6	1-5	0-4
Outturn	*£M3*	*19.4*	*12.8*	*11.2*	*9.5*	*11.9*				
	M1			*12.4*	*14.0*					
	PSL2			*11.6*	*12.6*					
	MO					*5.6*				

Table 2.3: The MTFS and the PSBR/GDP ratio

Targets/ projections set on:	80/1	81/2	82/3	83/4	84/5	85/6	86/7	87/8	88/9
26 Mar 80	3¾	3	2¼	1½					
10 Mar 81		4¼	3¼	2					
9 Mar 82			3½	2¾	2				
15 Mar 83				2¾	2½	2			
13 Mar 84					2¼	2	2	1¾	1¾
19 Mar 85						2	2	1¾	1¾
Outturn	*5.4*	*3.3*	*3.1*	*3.2*	*3.2*				

Paper on Monetary Control[4] had pointed out that 'no single statistical measure of the money supply can be expected fully to encapsulate monetary conditions, and so provide a uniquely correct basis for controlling the complex relationships between monetary growth and prices and nominal incomes'. Nevertheless, on grounds of clarity, it was thought appropriate to formulate monetary targets on the basis of one single aggregate, £M3. The use of more than one monetary aggregate for targetry was considered

Figure 2.1: Recorded £M3 and the targets, April 1977 to April 1985

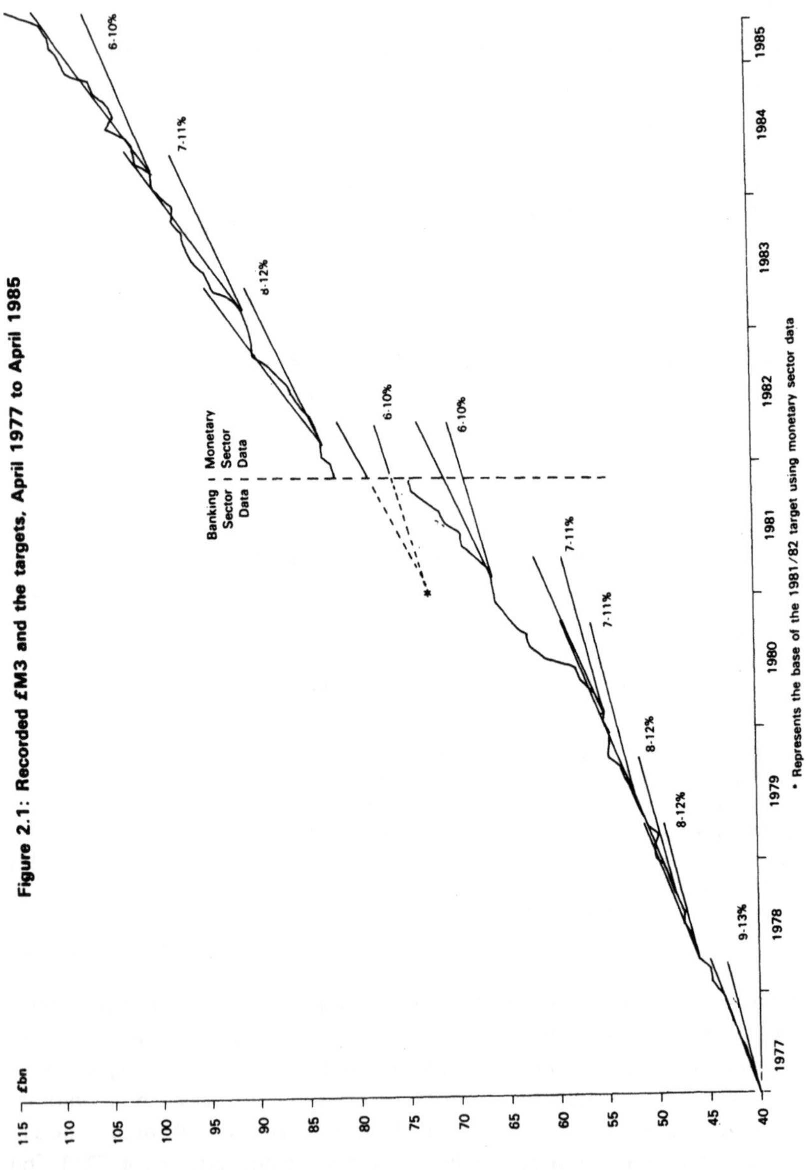

* Represents the base of the 1981/82 target using monetary sector data

inappropriate as it 'would make it much more difficult for the market and the public to appraise the determination of the authorities to meet their monetary objectives'[5].

The gradual movement of government policies away from 'Keynesian demand management' that had started in the mid-1970s, thus appeared to be completed. The post-war use of macro-economic policies to obtain full employment and micro-economic policies (various forms of price and wage restraint) to control inflation was overturned. Indeed, Lawson, commenting in 1984 on the MTFS said that it is the conquest of inflation, and not the pursuit of growth and employment, which is or should be the objective of macro-economic policy. And it is the creation of conditions conducive to growth and employment, and not the suppression of price rises, which is or should be the objective of micro-economic policy'[6].

Although the statement of the objectives of the MTFS changed only marginally between 1980/81 and 1985/86, the presentation of monetary policy in the achievement of such objectives was substantially revised. As noted above, the 1980/81 MTFS stated that the government's objectives for the medium term were to bring down inflation and to create conditions for sustainable growth of output and employment. The same statement of policy continued to be made throughout the life of the MTFS. In 1984/85, however, a change of detail was made: the government's 'ultimate objective' became the achievement of 'stable prices with lower interest rates'. Thus the rate of inflation was to fall to zero, and a reduction in interest rates in itself became an objective.

Difficulties with using £M3 as the chosen measure of money to target were encountered very soon after the 1980 Budget. The abolition of the 'corset' in June 1980 led to a substantial increase in £M3. In July and August the increase was 6½%, compared with a target rate of growth of 7-11% for the year as a whole. In the 1981/82 *FSBR* it was considered that '£M3 has not been a good indicator of monetary conditions in the past year'. Nevertheless, £M3 was retained as the sole target monetary aggregate. There appeared to be three main reasons for this. First, its velocity was thought to be stable in the medium term: the fast growth in relation to money GDP in 1980/81 (see Figure 2.2) could be considered a temporary aberration. Second, through the 'counterparts relationship' (see Chapter 3), £M3 could be linked to the stance of fiscal policy, the extent to which the fiscal deficit was financed by sales of debt to the non-bank private sector, the private sector's credit demand and external flows. Third, £M3 was well understood in financial markets.

In coming to the conclusion that financial conditions had been tight in 1980/81, the government looked at four other indicators. First, other mea-

Figure 2.2: Velocity of £M3

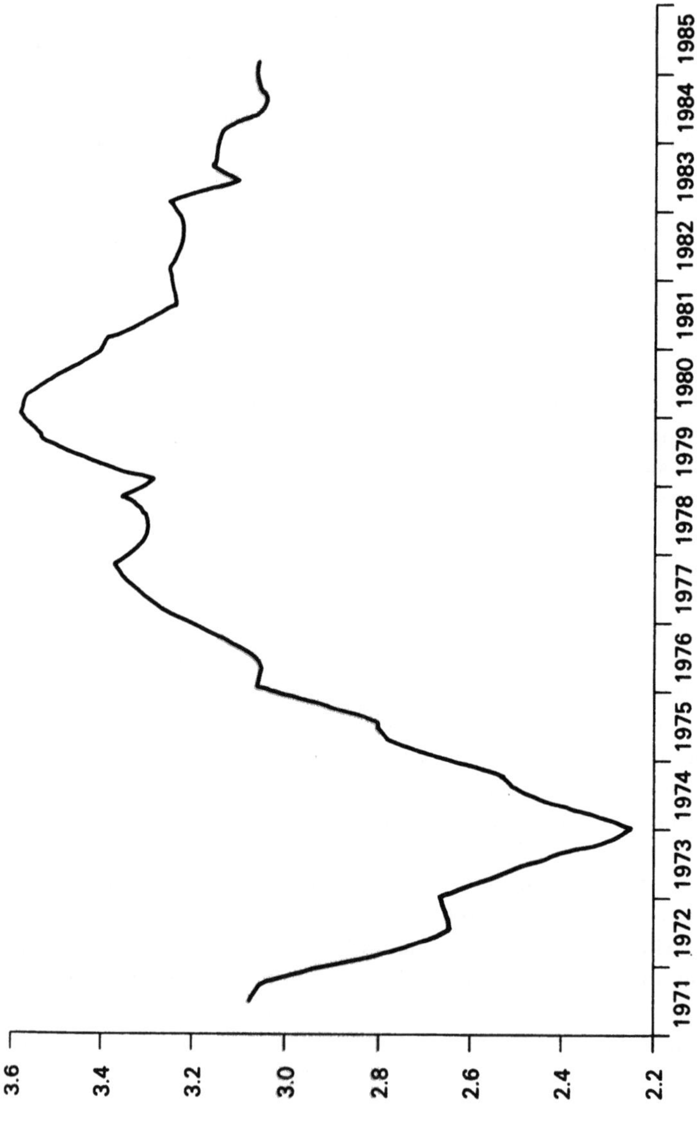

Ratio of Nominal GDP at market prices to the stock of £M3.

sures of money: it was noted that narrow money had fallen in real terms and that PSL1 (which includes private sector holdings of bills as well as money and was less distorted by the removal of the 'corset') had grown more slowly than £M3. Second, the exchange rate had been particularly strong, reaching peak levels of $2.45 to the £ on 4th November 1980 and 105 on the effective exchange rate index (1980=100) on 28th January 1981. Third, interest rates had been high and, fourth, there had not been 'any marked upward movement in the prices of houses or other real assets' (*FSBR*, 1981/82).

In the next financial year (1981/82) £M3 again grew rapidly — well above the top of its target range. The 1982/83 *FSBR* highlighted three factors which had made interpretation of £M3's behaviour particularly difficult. First, £M3 (as well as other monetary aggregates) had been affected by 'innovations and structural changes in financial markets'. The abolition of the 'corset' and the removal of exchange controls had been important influences on bank behaviour: for example, the banks started to lend on a significant scale for residential mortgages. Second, the demand for liquid balances as a means of saving appeared to increase. These two factors had tended to reduce the velocity of £M3, by around 4% in 1981/82. Third, the civil service dispute had seriously disrupted the pattern of financial flows in the economy, making interpretation of £M3 and its counterparts more difficult.

In this difficult environment, other indicators of the stance of policy were again taken into consideration. The behaviour of narrow money and nominal GDP, high real interest rates and weak asset prices were all considered as indicating that monetary conditions had remained restrictive.

The year had, however, seen the first of a series of exchange rate crises. In the Autumn of 1981 the authorities became seriously concerned about the decline in sterling's exchange rate and initiated a sharp rise in interest rates. The reasoning behind the move was set out in the December 1981 *BEQB*:

> ... the authorities were concerned that a further fall in the exchange rate, following the decline that had already taken place earlier in the year, would have serious adverse implications for inflation. Failure to respond rapidly to downward pressure on sterling appeared likely to risk accelerating sterling's fall, and a rise in the general level of short term interest rates therefore seemed appropriate.

In the light of the structural changes in the banking system and the increased desire to hold liquid balances as savings media, the target range for monetary growth was set at 8-12% for 1982/83, some 2 percentage points higher than the illustrative range for that period set down in the previous Budget. Moreover, the range was to apply to M1 and PSL2 as well as £M3 (see section (iii)). Growth of the monetary aggregates at the centre of this range (10%) would be equivalent to the anticipated rise in nominal GDP, leaving velocity unchanged. It was again stressed that the 'interpretation of monetary conditions will continue to take account of all the available evidence, including the behaviour of the exchange rate' (*FSBR*, 1982/83).

The explicit use of *three* target monetary aggregates was a departure from previous practice, apparently contradicting the view of the 1980 Green Paper on the desirability of using just one aggregate for reasons of clarity.

Nominal GDP grew much more slowly than expected in 1982/83 (7½% compared with a 1982 Budget forecast of 10%) as inflation turned out lower than forecast. Retail price inflation fell sharply — from 10.4% per annum at the time of the 1982 Budget to 4.6% per annum at the time of the 1983 Budget. Thus, even with a continued fall in velocity, £M3 finished the year within its target range. PSL2 grew at the upper end of, and M1 slightly above, the target range. The Chancellor was, therefore, able to claim in his 1983 Budget speech that monetary conditions had developed broadly as intended. Despite this, other indicators of the stance of monetary policy gave less convincing evidence of restrictive conditions. In particular, the end of 1982 had seen another sharp fall in the value of sterling, leading to some reversal of the fall in interest rates during the year. Base rates rose from 9% to 10/10¼% on 26th November 1982 and then again to 11% on 12th January (Appendix 1 gives details of the changes in official interest rates).

The same three monetary aggregates were targetted in 1983/84, with a common range (7-11%) that was one percentage point lower than in the previous year. Again the authorities would 'continue to take account of all the available evidence including the exchange rate, structural changes in financial markets, savings behaviour, and the level and structure of interest rates' (*FSBR*, 1983/84) when assessing monetary conditions. £M3 grew well within the target range during the year but PSL2 and M1 were above the range. It had been considered when M1 was introduced as a target monetary aggregate in the 1982 Budget, that lower interest rates and inflation might lead to rather faster growth in that aggregate: the 'cost' of holding M1 deposits (which were predominantly non-interest bearing) fell as interest rates fell and so demand for M1 might be expected to be correspondingly higher. The fast growth of M1, however, appeared to be due less to this factor than to the growing share of interest bearing deposits within the M1 measure: again, this was due to structural change in the banking system (see Chapter 4). PSL2 had grown rapidly due to the attractiveness of building society deposit rates.

The continuing problems associated with interpretation of the monetary aggregates had been highlighted in the reappraisal of monetary policy carried out in the Autumn of 1983. After the re-election of the Conservative government in June 1983, Nigel Lawson, the new Chancellor of the Exchequer, initiated a review of the MTFS. In particular, the question of the choice of target aggregates was addressed once more. The upshot of the reappraisal seemed to be a renewed emphasis on the use of monetary aggregates as intermediate targets of policy, with something of a move away from the more pragmatic approach which had developed over the previous three years. The preliminary results of the review were announced in Lawson's 'Mansion House Speech' in October 1983[7]. On the fundamental question of the ability of monetary aggregates to predict future inflation, it was now considered that narrow monetary aggregates were better predictors than broad aggregates — a finding at variance with the conventional wisdom of the 1970s. Moreover, it was thought that the demand for M0 was stable and predictable — i.e. it bore a reasonably close relationship to developments in nominal GDP — and that it could be controlled by variations in short term interest rates. The three essential attributes of a monetary aggregate which is suitable for targetry — that it predicts future inflation, has a stable velocity and can be controlled by the authorities — seemed to be possessed by M0. Although £M3 was still considered important, it was thought that it might be more useful in guiding the authorities' funding policy than in giving the signals for setting short term interest rates (see Chapter 5).

In both the 1984 and 1985 Budgets, M0 and £M3 were given equal weight in the assessment of monetary conditions. Separate target ranges were set for the aggregates, with M0's range two percentage points lower than that for £M3, reflecting historical differences in the trends of velocity of the two aggregates. Perhaps because of the greater emphasis placed on the attainment of lower interest rates as an objective in itself, the first eighteen months of the Conservatives' second term of office saw two more exchange rate crises — in July 1984 and January 1985. In both, a sharp rise in interest rates occurred as a result of exchange rate weakness. Following this, the 1985 Budget placed renewed emphasis on the behaviour of the exchange rate as an indicator of the stance of policy. That Budget also made clearer the government's forecasts for nominal GDP in the medium term, presenting these alongside the projections for monetary growth. The factors currently taken into account by the authorities in the assessment of the stance of policy are discussed in detail in Chapter 5.

(iii) Measures of money in the UK

Until the 1982 Budget, targets were set for just one monetary aggregate. Initially this was M3 but, from December 1976, attention was switched to £M3. Of course, no single aggregate can fully encapsulate all the available information on monetary conditions, and it would be irrational for the authorities to disregard all but one aggregate. Explicit recognition of this came in the 1982 Budget when the target ranges set for monetary growth in the year ahead were designed to apply to both broad and narrow measures of money: £M3 (and PSL2) and M1. The same aggregates were targetted in the next financial year. In the 1984 Budget, however, two separate target ranges were set: one for broad money (£M3) and one for narrow money (MO). In turn, PSL2 and M2 were to be monitored as the primary alternatives to these two aggregates when assessing broad and narrow money conditions respectively.

As many as eight monetary and liquidity aggregates are subjected to close scrutiny by the authorities: MO; M1 (and its non-interest bearing component, nib M1); M2; M3; £M3; PSL1; and PSL2. The PSL aggregates are often distinguished from the monetary aggregates; and the 'narrow' aggregates (the first four) from the 'broad' aggregates (the latter four). Generally, the narrow aggregates are more closely related to the use of money for transactions purposes whilst the broader aggregates include also assets more likely to be used for savings and investment. Figures 2.3 and 2.4 show the relationship between these various monetary and liquidity aggregates and their components.

Narrow Money

All of the monitored aggregates include notes and coin in circulation with the public, perhaps the most liquid of financial assets. MO, the authorities' targetted measure of narrow money, adds also the cash which banks hold in their tills and bankers' balances at the Bank of England. As such it includes (most of) the monetary liabilities of the Bank of England and has been termed the 'wide monetary base'. Narrower measures of the monetary base would include just bankers' operational deposits at the Bank of England or these deposits plus banks' till money. The monetary base is viewed to be of special importance by some economists and various methods of 'monetary base control' have been suggested (see Chapter 4). As Table 2.4 shows, notes and coin in circulation with the public form by far the largest proportion of M0. Chequable (or 'sight') bank deposits are

Table 2.4: Monetary aggregates: stocks, mid-April 1985

	£bn
Narrow measures	
Notes and coin in circulation with the public	12.4
M0	14.1
nib M1	33.9
M1	52.5
M2	136.9
Broad measures	
Sterling M3	113.8
Total M3	132.2
PSL1	118.5
PSL2	200.5

also readily accepted for making transactions. Adding such deposits to notes and coin in circulation gives the measure of money M1. Sight deposits can, however, conveniently be split into those which bear interest and those which do not. Excluding those which bear interest from M1 gives a measure of money called non interest bearing (or nib) M1. Many sight deposits which are interest bearing can, however, readily be used for making transactions (for example, the recently introduced high interest bearing cheque accounts, which have proved popular with the personal sector, are highly liquid). Thus in the specially designed measure of transactions balances, M2, the Bank includes certain of these interest bearing deposits. When deciding on the types of deposits to include in M2, three factors were taken into account[8]. First, to be suitable for transactions, a deposit must have reasonably short *maturity*. Second, in an attempt to exclude deposits which are used primarily for investment rather than transactions purposes, a limit on the *size* of deposits included in the aggregate should be placed. Any size distinction is, however, obviously arbitrary. Third, the *type of deposit* should be taken into account. In particular, for a deposit to be suitable for transactions, it should be transferable to third parties on demand or at short notice.

Figure 2.3: Relationships among the narrow monetary aggregates and their components

Notes and coin in circulation with the public	
	plus Banks' till money
	plus Bankers' operational balances with the Bank of England
	equals **Wide monetary base (M0)**
plus Private sector non-interest bearing sterling sight bank deposits	
equals **Non-interest bearing component of M1**	
	plus Private sector interest-bearing retail sterling bank deposits
	plus Private sector holdings of retail building society deposits and NSB ordinary accounts
	equals **M2**
plus Private sector interest-bearing sterling sight bank deposits	
equals **M1**	

Figure 2.4: Relationships among the broad monetary and liquidity aggregates and their components

M1

plus Private sector sterling time bank deposits — original maturity of up to two years

plus Private sector holdings of sterling bank certificates of deposit

plus Private sector sterling time bank deposits — original maturity of over two years

equals **Sterling M3**

plus Private sector foreign currency bank deposits

equals **Total M3**

plus Private sector holdings of money market instruments (bank bills, Treasury bills, local authority deposits) and certificates of tax deposit

equals **PSL1**

plus Private sector holdings of building society deposits (excluding term shares and SAYE) and National Savings instruments (excluding certificates, SAYE and other longer term deposits)

less Building society holdings of money market instruments, bank deposits, etc.

equals **PSL2**

The balance of these considerations led to the following components being included in the M2 measure:

(a) notes and coin in circulation with the public and non-interest bearing sight bank deposits;
(b) all other deposits on which cheques may be drawn or from which standing orders, direct debit mandates and other payments to third parties may be made;
(c) other deposits of less than £100,000 having a residual maturity of less than one month.

Only deposits denominated in sterling and held by the private sector are included. Both bank and building society deposits which satisfy the criteria are included, as well as deposits in the National Savings Bank Ordinary Account (Chapter 7 discusses types of National Savings in detail).

Public sector deposits are now excluded from all measures of money in the UK[9]. Before February 1984, £M3 and M3 included such deposits. Their level was small, although often erratic, and not related in any meaningful way to economic developments. Their exclusion brought the definition of UK monetary aggregates into line with the definitions in other countries.

The four measures discussed above — M0, nib M1, M1 and M2 — are the primary measures of narrow money examined by the authorities. In both the 1984/85 and 1985/86 strategies, M0 was targetted with M2 acting as the most important secondary indicator of narrow money developments (the properties of M0 are examined fully in Chapter 4). Although M2 is perhaps the most satisfactory measure of transactions balances, a more central role for it is largely ruled out for the present time by the short run of data available. Data are only available from November 1981 onwards: this precludes seasonal adjustment and assessment of the relationship between M2 and other economic variables. Furthermore, some three quarters of M2 is interest bearing and it has recently behaved more like a measure of broad money. In 1984/85, interpretation of its behaviour was rendered difficult by the changes in the terms of some building society accounts.

Broad Money

There are also four closely watched measures of broad money (see Figure 2.4). *£M3* is by far the best known. It adds to M1 all UK private sector holdings of sterling time deposits and certificates of deposit (CDs). When monetary targets were first set, *total M3* was the target aggregate: this adds to £M3 the UK private sector's foreign currency bank deposits.

After only five months as the target aggregate, however, it was decided (in December 1976) to replace M3 with £M3 as the target aggregate. An important consideration in the decision was the fact that UK residents could, at that time, only hold foreign currency deposits for purposes approved by the exchange control authorities. When exchange controls were in force, the large bulk of these foreign currency deposits were known to be related to transactions by the holders in goods and services in other countries: they were not likely to be particularly closely related to economic activity in the UK. It is still probably true that this remains the case, although UK residents have, since the abolition of exchange controls, used such deposits for investment as well as transactions purposes.

Another reason for excluding foreign currency deposits from the chosen target measure of money supply is that their sterling capital value is uncertain (unless they are covered in the forward market). Indeed, if a substantial number of holders switched out of foreign currency deposits and into sterling, they could generate a movement in the exchange rate against themselves. A further reason is that foreign currency deposits with banks abroad are not included in the UK monetary aggregates, even though, to the holder, there may be little difference between these deposits and those held with the UK monetary sector.

Although the introduction of the new 'monetary' sector, in place of the 'banking' sector at the end of 1981, increased the number of banks whose deposits were included in the measurement of £M3, a number of other deposit taking institutions continued to be excluded, most notably the building societies. It might be argued that it is anomalous for deposits with the UK office of a small foreign bank to be included in £M3, whereas deposits with a UK building society are excluded. Moreover, monetary institutions which are included in the UK monetary sector can provide services which are effectively intermediation facilities, but which are not included on their balance sheets and therefore not included in £M3. For example, a bank can accept a commercial bill which is then taken up by the non-bank sector, thereby providing credit for a company and a liquid, marketable asset to a saver. This accepted commercial bill or bank bill has almost identical characteristics to a certificate of deposit issued by a bank, but only the latter is included in £M3. The level of bank bills held by the non-bank sector is called the 'bill leak'. Although this form of substitute intermediation occurs off the balance sheet of the bank (the loan is a contingent liability of the bank), it would appear that the economic implications are almost identical to that of direct deposit taking and lending. Switches between on and off-balance sheet forms of intermediation, possibly as a result of direct controls on banks' balance sheets, may result in the consolidated balance sheet of the UK monetary sector giving a misleading indication of monetary conditions. Deposit taking and credit lines can also be extended to UK residents, either in sterling or in foreign currencies by banks outside the UK monetary sector, whose balance sheets are not included in the measurement of £M3.

The problems identified above were particularly acute during the periods in which the 'corset' was applied to the banking sector. This scheme, which imposed penalties on banks for expanding their interest bearing eligible liabilities faster than a certain rate, encouraged the 'bill leak' and (especially once exchange controls had been removed) the channelling of business through subsidiaries of UK banks (not included in the UK banking sector). The balance sheets of UK banks included within the banking sector thus appeared to show them performing less intermediation: the term 'cosmetic disintermediation' was developed to describe the process. When the 'corset' controls were removed a large expansion of banks' balance sheets occurred as the business was 're-intermediated.' (i.e. brought back within the banking sector's balance sheet).

The public sector may behave like a banking institution by raising credit for itself (or for on-lending to the private sector) or issuing liquid debt instruments such as Treasury bills, National Savings and Certificates of Tax Deposit. Non-bank holdings of these debt instruments may be as liquid as the non-banks' claims on the UK monetary sector; for example a Treasury bills is as liquid, if not more so, than a certificate of deposit issued by a bank. Thus, £M3 does not encompass all intermediation or substitute intermediation facilities provided to UK residents, nor does it include all types of asset which have monetary or near-monetary characteristics.

The liquidity aggregates (PSL1 and PSL2) go some way to correcting these problems. These measures include all the components of £M3 apart from those sterling time deposits held by the UK private sector with an original maturity of over two years. Such deposits are not regarded as particularly liquid, being more likely to be related to long term savings balances. PSL1 adds to the modified measure of £M3 the size of the 'bill leak' and the level of UK private sector holdings of Treasury bills, local authority deposits and certificates of tax deposits (CTDs). PSL2 adds to PSL1 most building society deposits and National Savings. Again, however, those components which are not thought particularly liquid are excluded. Thus building society term shares and SAYE, National Savings Certificates and other longer term deposits are not included. As M2 and PSL2 are the only aggregates which include building society deposits, there are some grounds for treating them separately. This concept of 'symmetry' appears to have been important in the choice of M0 and £M3 as target aggregates and M2 and PSL2 as the most important secondary indicators of monetary developments in the 1984 Budget.

All the components of money and liquidity differ in the extent to which they are liquid and hence suitable for making transactions. Generally, one would expect the narrower definitions of money to comprise of assets used predominantly for transactions purposes whereas the broader measures would add assets more likely to be used as savings instruments. Partly because of this, there must be some uncertainty about the appropriateness of simple sum aggregation (ie. adding all the components of the monetary aggregate together with weights of unity). More suitable, perhaps, would be to weight the different assets according to the extent to which they are used for transactions purposes. Measures of the turnover of different asset types could provide an indication of this. Alternatively the 'user cost' (essentially the difference between the return on the asset and that on a high yielding competing asset) could be used. Conceptually, all monetary components could be used in such a measure, with weights declining as the components become less 'money like'[10].

One of the continuing attractions of targetting a 'broad' aggregate, such as £M3, rather than a narrow aggregate is the accounting identity linkage between £M3 and the authorities' budgetary, financial and exchange rate policies. Strictly speaking there is an accounting identity linkage between all the monetary aggregates and their flow of fund counterparts, but targets for 'narrow' aggregates can be met by what may be 'cosmetic' adjustments to banks' balance sheets. For instance, it might be possible to meet an M1 target solely by readjustments to the composition of banks' balance sheets (for example, switches between sight and time deposits) without any significant adjustments to the flow of funds in the non-bank sectors. Whereas the value of targets for narrow aggregates depends on the stability of an econometric relationship, targets for 'broad' aggregates can be justified in terms of their accounting identity relationship. The next chapter discusses the analysis of broad money in this manner more fully.

(iv) The calculation of monetary targets

The method of calculation of monetary targets has changed from time to time. Since 1980, two methods have been used. The first, used for the period 1980/81 to 1984/85 calculated monetary growth by reference to the annualised rate of growth since the start of the target period. The second, used for 1985/86, calculates monetary growth on the basis of a twelve month growth rate[11].

The old method of calculation defined the target period as the fourteen months from banking February in one year to banking April of the next year. (The period was chosen as one which encompassed the financial year). The growth of the monetary aggregates was presented as the annualised rate of growth since the start of the target period. The main drawback with this approach was that a progressively larger number of months' growth was taken into account when assessing the growth rate since the start of the target period. Thus, erratically high growth at the start of the period would give a very high annualised growth rate: as the target period progressed, each additional month's item of data carried a progressively smaller weight in the calculation of the annualised growth rate.

The new method of calculation, by looking at the twelve month growth rate, avoids this problem as each additional month's data carries equal weight. A twelve month growth rate responds, however, only relatively slowly to changes in trend. Annualised growth rates over the last three and six months, also published regularly by the Bank do, however, help in the assessment of any tendency for the aggregates to accelerate or decelerate.

Targets apply for the financial year, with the twelve months from banking March to banking March taken as the closest approximation to this period. There is thus no 'overlapping' period as there was with the old fourteen month range.

With both methods of calculation, the target ranges are set for seasonally adjusted monetary aggregates since the authorities wish to control the underlying rate of growth rather than offset seasonal variations. (The method of seasonal adjustment is described in more detail in Chapter 3). Because the seasonal pattern for each year is not recurrent and the seasonals are constrained to sum to zero over an annual period, the month-on-month change in the seasonally adjusted levels series for the monetary aggregates (Table 11.1, *BEQB*) are not the same as the flows series (Table 11.2, *BEQB*). For example, in the August 1983 *Banking Statistics*[12], the seasonally adjusted change in £M3 for August 1983 was +£152 million. The levels of seasonally adjusted £M3 in July and August 1983 were 98,300 and 98,420 respectively, a change of +£120 million.

When calculating the percentage rate of growth of seasonally adjusted monetary aggregates, it is conventional to cumulate the seasonally adjusted flows and take them as a percentage of a seasonally adjusted level. An example of the calculation of the twelve month growth rate is given in Table 2.5.

Table 2.5: Construction of target period growth rates for £M3

	Level (s.a.)	Flow (s.a.)	Cumulative flow	% change since Feb '84	Annualised % change since Feb '84
February 1984	99740				
March		1382	1382	1.39	18.0
April		366	1748	1.75	11.0
May		858	2606	2.61	10.9
June		2075	4681	4.69	14.8
July		-1025	3656	3.67	9.0
August		739	4395	4.41	9.0
September		1365	5760	5.78	10.1
October		319	6079	6.09	9.3
November		2809	8888	8.91	12.1
December		-535	8353	8.37	10.1
January 1985		760	9113	9.14	10.0
February		531	9644	9.67	9.7
March		1147	10791	10.82	9.9
April		3173	13964	14.00	11.9

One advantage of using this method is that it reduces the problem of breaks in the series, which can occur during a target period. Breaks can arise as a result of the inclusion or exclusion of particular institutions from the UK monetary sector.

Although seasonal adjustment smooths the £M3 series to some extent, sizeable random fluctuations can occur in any one month. Over a number of months these fluctuations will tend to cancel each other out and, therefore, the annualised rate of growth over several months will give some indication of the underlying rate of growth. The authorities, for example, currently present the three and six month annualised growth rates alongside the twelve month growth rate in the monthly *Banking Statistics* Press Release.

With the old method of calculating annualised rates of growth from a base period, if £M3 overshot its target range in any particular period, the question arose of whether to accommodate the overshoot. *Base drift* occurs if a new target is re-based on an outturn which is above the mid-point of the previous target range. As discussed above, base drift has been tolerated (see Figure 2.1). In the 1981/82 *FSBR*, however, it was stated that 'it is the Government's intention to consider clawing back some of the past year's rapid growth of £M3 by permitting an undershoot as and when the opportunity arises'. The problem does not arise with the new method of calculation as the growth rates are no longer defined by reference to a base period.

Notes and References

1. J. S. Fforde, 'Setting Monetary Objectives', *BEQB*, June 1983, p203.
2. *BEQB*, December 1977, p437.
3. J. S. Fforde, op.cit., p203.
4. 'Monetary Control', Command 7858, (London: HMSO, 1980), p.iii.
5. 'Monetary Control', op.cit., p.iv.
6. N. Lawson, 'The Fifth Mais Lecture. The British Experience', (H.M. Treasury, 19 June 1984).
7. N. Lawson, 'The Chancellor's Mansion House Speech', (H.M. Treasury, 20 October 1983).
8. See 'Transactions Balances — a new monetary aggregate', *BEQB*, June 1982, pp.224-5.
9. See 'Changes to monetary aggregates and the analysis of bank lending', *BEQB*, March 1984, pp.78-83.
10. For a full discussion of this matter see T. C. Mills, 'Composite monetary indicators for the United Kingdom; construction and empirical analysis', *Bank of England Discussion Papers*, Technical Series No. 3 (May 1983).
11. H.M. Treasury, 'Economic Progress Report', (May 1985).
12. *Banking Statistics* is a monthly publication by the Bank of England which gives new data relating to some of the tables in the *BEQB*.

3 Analysing Broad Money

The central purpose of this chapter is to explain the way in which the authorities analyse developments in broad measures of money. As explained in the last chapter, £M3 has been the measure of broad money targetted by the authorities since 1976. It is the analysis of that particular aggregate which is given most attention in this chapter.

£M3 comprises notes and coin in circulation with the public and those sterling deposits (both sight and time) of the UK private sector with the UK monetary sector ('banks' for short). These deposits form part of the total liabilities of the monetary sector; its other liabilities are deposits denominated in other currencies, sterling deposits of sectors other than the private sector and non-deposit liabilities. By definition, total liabilities must equal total assets: banks' assets consist mainly of loans to other sectors of the economy. As banks' balance sheets must balance, the level of deposits included within £M3 can be expressed as the difference between the banks' total assets and those liabilities in the balance sheet which are not included in the measurement of £M3.

Both sides of the banks' balance sheet are subject to change by the actions of other sectors of the economy. For example, banks may receive new deposits (say, as the personal sector switches money from building society accounts to the banks), or customers may decide to draw down on overdraft facilities, thus increasing the banks' lending. Banks will adjust their balance sheets in order to accommodate such changes.

The process whereby the banks adjust their deposit rates in order to bring their liabilities into line with their assets is known as liability management. The process whereby the banks adjust their lending rates and conditions in order to keep their assets side in line with their liabilities is known as asset management. Clearly asset and liability management can, and do, occur simultaneously. However, at least since the late 1960s, and particularly since the inauguration of competition and credit control in 1971, liability management appears to have dominated asset management. In particular, deposit creation by the banks appears to have been primarily determined by the demand for credit, rather than the supply of credit being determined by the non-banks' willingness to make deposits with the banks. Expressing £M3 in terms of its 'asset counterparts' (i.e. the assets of the banks net of those liabilities not included in the measurement of £M3) enables this relationship to be expressed more clearly.

The public sector may borrow from the banks in order to finance its deficit. In many ways, however, this is a residual form of finance for the public sector. Bank lending to the public sector may be expressed as the difference between the public sector's borrowing requirement (PSBR) and all other sources of finance (apart from borrowing from the banks). Thus this element in the banks' balance sheet can be replaced by its 'counterparts'.

In this way the relationship between £M3 and its counterparts is built up. The relationship is a central feature of the Bank of England's monthly *Banking Statistics* and forms the basis for most commentary on the behaviour of this monetary aggregate. The next three sections explain in detail how this counterparts relationship is built up: to start, the nature of the balance sheet of the monetary sector as a whole is examined; then the way in which the PSBR is financed is analysed; and finally the counterparts relationship is developed. The following two sections then discuss the nature of counterpart movements, examining in detail the determinants of both the 'domestic' and 'external' counterparts.

(i) Consolidated balance sheet of the UK monetary sector

Table 6 in the *BEQB* is a consolidated balance sheet of the UK monetary sector which comprises:

a) all recognised banks and licensed deposit-taking institutions (LDTs)
b) the National Girobank
c) the trustee savings banks
d) the Banking Department of the Bank of England
e) those banks in the Channel Islands and the Isle of Man which have chosen to comply with the current monetary control arrangements.

BEQB Table 3.1 provides a summary of the balance sheets of those institutions in the monetary sector which report monthly (generally those with a total balance sheet size of £100 million or more, or eligible liabilities of £10 million or more) other than the discount houses. The adjustments made in *BEQB* Table 6 to net out interbank transactions and transit items (see below) are not made in *BEQB* Table 3. There are seven categories of banks included in *BEQB* Table 3:

Retail banks (*BEQB* Table 3.2) which comprises banks which either have extensive branch networks in the UK or participate directly in the UK clearing system. It includes those branches in the Channel Islands and the Isle of Man which the parent bank has opted to include within the UK monetary control arrangements and thus within the UK monetary sector;
Accepting Houses (*BEQB* Table 3.3) which comprises the members of the Accepting Houses Committee (and certain subsidiaries);
American banks (*BEQB* Table 3.5);
Japanese banks (*BEQB* Table 3.6);
Other overseas banks (*BEQB* 3.7);
Consortium banks (*BEQB* Table 3.8) which comprises UK registered institutions which are owned by banks or financial institutions but in which no one institution has a direct share holding of more than 50%, and in which at least one share holder is based overseas;
Other domestic and overseas banks (*BEQB* Table 3.6 and *BEQB* Table 3.9).

The figures in *BEQB* Table 6 are designed to show the position of the banks in relation to third parties ('non-banks'); transactions between institutions within the sector ('interbank' transactions) are netted out. In general netting out interbank transactions is appropriate in order to assess the impact of the UK banking system on the rest of the economy. The non-banks are categorised into the UK public sector (central government, local government and public corporations), the UK non-bank private sector (industrial and commercial companies, the personal sector, other financial institutions) and the non-resident or overseas sector. Interbank transactions are netted out on consolidation as illustrated below in Table 3.1.

Although each bank submits a balance sheet which has to be internally consistent, misreporting of interbank transactions may give rise to an interbank difference on consolidation: the total of all reported interbank loans may not be equal to the total of all reported interbank deposits. A (global) adjustment is made to the net non-deposit liabilities item in the consolidated balance sheet to allow for any such discrepancy in sterling items while the adjustment for a discrepancy in foreign currency items is made to the overseas sector's foreign currency deposits. The month-to-month change in the interbank difference is impossible to forecast accurately: it may be a sizeable factor in the overall non-deposit liabilities figure in individual months, but over longer periods it tends to cancel out.

Cheque clearing, other than Town clearing, usually takes about three days. If no adjustment were to be made for delays in interbank settlement, simple aggregation of banks' balance sheets would give rise to double-counting: uncleared cheques (or standing orders) credited to (or debited

Table 3.1: Consolidation of two banks' balance sheets

Bank A				**Bank B**			
Liabilities		*Assets*		*Liabilities*		*Assets*	
non-bank deposits	150	Loans to non-banks	50	non-bank deposits	50	Loans to non-banks	150
		Loans to Bank B	100	Bank A's deposits	100		
	150		**150**		**150**		**150**

Consolidated Balance Sheet of A and B

Liabilities		*Assets*	
non-bank deposits	200	Loans to non-banks	200
	200		**200**

from) customers' accounts at close of business on the reporting day would not be offset by corresponding adjustments to the balance sheets of other banks. A simple example employing two banks can be used to illustrate the problem of double-counting due to transit items. On day 1 (see Table 3.2) no transactions take place and the consolidated balance sheet total is just the sum of the two individual balance sheet totals.

Table 3.2: Influence of transit items; day 1

Bank A				**Bank B**			
Liabilities		*Assets*		*Liabilities*		*Assets*	
non-bank deposits	100	non-bank loans	100	non-bank deposits	100	non-bank loans	100
	100		**100**		**100**		**100**

On day 2 (Table 3.3) the customers of bank B present cheques drawn on the customers of bank A to a value of 20. Also, the customers of bank B have standing orders of value 10 payable to the customers of bank A which are due for payment on day 2. If, on average, bank customers respond to a receipt or a payment by adjusting their deposits and bank borrowing in the ratio 60:40 respectively, the cheque of 20 due to the customers of bank B will raise deposit liabilities by 12 to 112 and reduce lending by 8 to 92. The uncleared cheque of 20 will be an asset of bank B (Items in Collection).

Table 3.3: Influence of transit items; Day 2

Bank A				**Bank B**			
Liabilities		*Assets*		*Liabilities*		*Assets*	
non-bank deposits	100	non-bank loans	100	non-bank deposits	106	non-bank loans	96
				Items in tr'mission	10	Items in collection	20
	100		**100**		**116**		**116**

The standing order of 10 will reduce deposits by 6 to 106 and raise lending by 4 to 96. The uncleared standing order will be a liability of bank B (Items in transmission). If no adjustment is made for transit items the balance sheet total for both the banks comes to 216. A properly consolidated balance sheet can be achieved if the net transit items of 20-10=10 are allocated on a 60:40 basis to the customers of bank A. (Table 3.4)

Table 3.4: Consolidated balance sheet allowing for transit items

Bank A				**Bank B**			
Liabilities		*Assets*		*Liabilities*		*Assets*	
non-bank deposits	100	non-bank loans	100	non-bank deposits	106	non-bank loans	96
	-6		4				

Consolidated Balance Sheet of A and B

Liabilities		*Assets*	
non-bank deposits	206	non-bank loans	196
	-6		4
	200		**200**

If this assumption about customers' behaviour is valid, double counting will be avoided. To the extent that the assumption is invalid, this method will yield an incorrect consolidated balance sheet total and an under or over-recording of sterling deposits and lending. In general net sterling transit items are sufficiently small not to cause excessive distortions to the published monetary figures. However, if for some reason cheque clearing is disrupted over a monthly make-up day and the 60:40 split is inappropriate, the published change over the month may be significantly distorted. A recent example of this problem occurred with the data for banking June 1985. On make up day, the bankers handling the sale of shares in Abbey Life Group PLC were in possession of about £4bn of returnable application money (the offer for sale having been substantially oversubscribed). This money was held in a suspense account which is treated, in the calculation of the monetary statistics, in the same way as a transit item. Thus 40% of the £4bn was subtracted from bank lending and 60% added to bank (non-interest bearing sight) deposits. If more than 40% of the returned money acts to reduce bank lending (and consequently less than 60% acts to raise bank deposits) then monetary growth will be overstated as a result of the application of the rule. The maximum upward distortion in this case was £2.4bn (i.e. 60% of £4bn) if all the returned money acted to reduce bank lending and none to increase deposits. On the other hand, if all the returned money acted to raise deposits, and none to reduce bank lending, monetary growth would be understated as a result of the application of the rule: in this case, the maximum understatement would be £1.6bn (i.e. 40% of £4bn).

Net foreign currency transit items are comparatively small: on consolidation they are amalgamated 100% with the overseas sector's foreign currency deposits.

Valuation of Foreign Currency Deposits and Lending

Each bank reports its foreign currency deposits and lending in terms of sterling converted at the appropriate middle closing spot price on make-up day. Any net revaluation difference between the sterling value of foreign currency assets and foreign currency liabilities resulting from a change in the spot price of foreign exchange automatically adds to non-deposit liabilities. For example, if a bank takes foreign currency deposits of $200 and switches half of them into sterling lending, its balance sheet may look like the one given in Table 3.5. The make-up day exchange rate is assumed to be $2.00 to £1.

Table 3.5: Balance sheet with foreign currency business; Month 1

Liabilities		*Assets*	
£ value of f/c deposits	100	£ value of f/c lending	50
£ deposits	50	£ lending	150
non-deposit liabilities	50		
	200		**200**

On make-up day the following month the sterling exchange rate is assumed to have risen to $4.00 to £1. If no transactions are made by the bank during the month, the balance sheet will change to that given in Table 3.6:

Table 3.6: Balance sheet with foreign currency business; Month 2

Liabilities		*Assets*	
£ value of f/c deposits	50	£ value of f/c lending	25
£ deposits	50	£ lending	150
non-deposit liabilities	75		
	175		**175**

The sterling value of foreign currency deposits is halved to 50 and foreign currency lending is halved to 25. The net revaluation diffence of 25 arising out of the change in the spot price represents the bank's gain on its net foreign currency position in spot terms, and in this accounting convention adds to non-deposit liabilities, raising them to 75. The reported month-to-month change in foreign currency assets and liabilities therefore reflects changes in the exchange rate as well as transactions in foreign currencies. The net revaluation difference within non-deposit liabilities represents a notional sterling profit or loss on foreign exchange transactions. In practice most foreign currency switch positions are covered, and therefore the profit or loss on foreign exchange will not necessarily bear much relation to changes in the spot price of sterling or, taking a longer perspective, to banks' profits. For this reason the covered rather than the uncovered interest rate differential may be an important factor influencing the banks' switch positions.

When presenting changes in balance sheet levels an attempt is made to exclude the effect of exchange rate changes so that changes in foreign currency items in *BEQB* Table 6 reflect only actual transactions in foreign currency by the UK banks. Using the example given in Tables 3.5 and 3.6, where the foreign currency items are known to be denominated in dollars, the adjusted sterling change in foreign currency items can be calculated according to the formula:

$$dT = (X_t e_t - X_{t-1} e_{t-1}) / \mathbf{e}_t$$

where:

dT = actual transactions in foreign currency items in terms of sterling, over the banking month

x_t = stock of foreign currency items at t in terms of sterling

e_t = appropriate exchange rate at t

$\mathbf{e}_t$ = daily average of appropriate exchange rate over the banking month

The sterling levels of foreign currency items are reconverted back into foreign currency values at the make-up day exchange rate. The change over the month is calculated and is then reconverted back into sterling by multiplying by the reciprocal of the daily average exchange rate. Thus, in the example, the adjusted change in foreign currency deposits is:

(50 x 4 - 100 x 2/daily average dollar exchange rate) = 0

The adjusted change in foreign currency lending is:

(25 x 4 - 50 x 2/daily average dollar exchange rate) = 0

Tables 3.5 and 3.6 were constructed on the assumption that no transactions took place. However, if transactions do take place, the reported balance sheet for month 2 could look like that given in Table 3.7.

Table 3.7: Balance sheet with foreign currency business, including transactions

Liabilities		*Assets*	
£ value of f/c deposits	75	£ value of f/c lending	50
£ deposits	50	£ lending	150
non-deposit liabilities	75		
	200		**200**

If the daily average exchange rate was 3.10, the adjusted change in foreign currency deposits would be (75 x 4 - 100 x 2)/3.10 = 32, and the adjusted change in foreign currency lending would be (50 x 4 - 50 x 2)/3.10 = 32. The balance sheet corresponding to the changes represented in *BEQB* Table 6 is given in Table 3.8.

The net revaluation difference of 25 which raises net non-deposit liabilities in Table 3.6 to 75 is cancelled out in Table 3.8. Since changes in foreign currency items due to changes in the exchange rate are supposed to be removed in Table 3.8, no net revaluation difference should arise.

Table 3.8: Balance sheet with foreign currency business, including revaluations

Liabilities		*Assets*	
£ value of f/c deposits	132	£ value of f/c lending	82
£ deposits	50	£ lending	150
non-deposit liabilities	50		
	232		**232**

If individual foreign currency components of the UK banks' consolidated balance sheet are known to be of a particular currency denomination, they are adjusted using the appropriate exchange rate. Otherwise, composite exchange rates are used, with weights which are based on the relative shares of the components in that currency. Errors in the adjustment of foreign currency items for changes in the exchange rate may arise because of incorrect weightings in the composite exchange rates. Also, the daily average exchange rate can only be an approximation to the conceptually correct, but unobservable, weighted average exchange rate, where the weights are the proportion of the transactions done at each exchange rate.

The components of the consolidated balance sheet of the UK monetary sector are shown in Table 3.9.

Table 3.9: Consolidated balance sheet of the UK monetary sector

Liabilities		*Assets*	
Public Sector Deposits		Lending to Public Sector	
- in Sterling	PUB£D	- in Sterling	PUB£L
- in other currencies	PUB$D	- in other currencies	PUB$L
Private Sector Deposits		Lending to Private Sector	
- in sterling	PRV£D	- in sterling	PRV£L
- in other currencies	PRV$D	- in other currencies	PRV$L
Overseas Sector Deposits		Lending to Overseas Sector	
- in sterling	OS£D	- in sterling	OS£L
- in other currencies	OS$D	- in other currencies	OS$L
Non-deposit Liabilities (Net)	NNDL		

(PUB£D+PUB$D+PRV£D+PRV$D+OS£D+OS$D+NNDL)
= (PUB£L+PUB$L+PRV£L+PRV$L+OS£L+OS$L) (1)

Table corresponds to *BEQB*, Table 6

For the balance sheet to balance, total assets must equal total liabilities (the relationship (1) shown at the bottom of the balance sheet); and the change (d) in total assets must equal the change in total liabilities:

d (PUB£D + PUB$D + PRV£D + PRV$D + OS£D + OS$D + NNDL) = d (PUB£L + PUB$L + PRV£L + PRV$L + OS£L + OS$L) (1a)

(ii) Financing the PSBR

The public sector finances its borrowing requirement by borrowing from the three other sectors of the economy: the non-bank private sector; the monetary sector; and the overseas sector. The types of debt which the public sector sells are described briefly in this section: in Chapter 7 a fuller description of the debt instruments is given (data on the financing of the PSBR are given in *FS* Table 2.6).

The *non-bank private sector* finances the PSBR in two main ways.

First, it can increase its holdings of notes and coin (dPRVNAC). The authorities respond passively to any change in the demand for notes and coin (cash). If the non-bank private sector increases its demand for cash, deposits at the banks are run down in exchange for cash and the banks' vault cash is reduced. The clearers then replenish their stocks of vault cash by running down their balances with the Bank of England in exchange for cash. An increase in the issue of notes will raise the liabilities of the Issue Department of the Bank of England, which in turn matches this increase in its liabilities by purchasing government securities. This will reduce the amount of debt which will need to be sold elsewhere to finance the PSBR.

Second, the non-bank private sector can purchase government debt (dPRV£G). This may be marketable (Treasury bills or gilts) or non-marketable (National Savings or certificates of tax deposit (CTDs)). Against this, if the Issue Department of the Bank of England buys commercial bills (dIDCB), the government needs to raise more from other sources. Thus Issue Department's net purchases of commercial bills enter the PSBR financing identity with a negative sign.

The public sector may also borrow from the *monetary sector*. This mainly takes the form of purchases of government debt (gilts or Treasury bills). The weekly purchase of Treasury bills by the discount houses (included in the monetary sector) was traditionally the method by which the government financed that part of its borrowing requirement which could not be financed elsewhere. (As explained in Chapter 6, however, this function has now largely disappeared). Any increase in the banks' holdings of notes and coin ('vault cash') also finances the PSBR. These forms of finance — purchase of government debt or an increase in vault cash — are collectively referred to as dPUB£L in the identity below. The banks may also lend to the public sector in foreign currencies (dPUB$L) or the public sector may run down its deposits with the banks (in either sterling, dPUB£D, or foreign currencies, dPUB$D) in order to finance its borrowing requirement. (Before the 1984/85 financial year, changes in the public sector's holdings of bank deposits were treated as contributing to, rather than financing, the PSBR).

In a similar manner, the *overseas sector*'s purchases of government debt, as well as an increase in its holdings of notes and coin, finance the PSBR (referred to as dOS£G below).

Foreign exchange intervention by the Exchange Equalisation Account (EEA) has a public sector financing counterpart. The EEA holds international reserves (RES) and short term sterling claims (mostly Treasury bills) on the public sector. If the EEA purchases foreign currencies in exchange for sterling, the sterling is raised by selling government debt. In this instance the EEA's international reserves rise and its sterling assets fall; as a result the public sector is forced to finance more of its borrowing requirement by some other means. If reserves increase because of official foreign currency borrowing, or through a new allocation of Special Drawing Rights, (OF$) the EEA does not have to sell Treasury bills in order to raise the sterling to purchase foreign currencies. As a result there is no change in the external financing component of the PSBR. Thus, the net domestic financing counterpart of official foreign exchange intervention is:

dRES - dPUB$L - dOF$

We can bring together all of these sources of finance in the equation below. In all cases, the relationship is between the PSBR and the change (d) in each of the financing components:

PSBR = dPRV£G
(sales of public sector debt to the UK non-bank private sector)
— dIDCB
(Issue Department's purchases of commercial bills)
\+ dPRVNAC
(increase in demand for notes and coin by the non-bank private sector)
\+ dPUB£L
(sterling lending to the public sector)
\+ dPUB$L
(foreign currency lending to the public sector)
— dPUB£D
(public sector sterling deposits)
— dPUB$D
(public sector foreign currency deposits)
— dRES
(international reserves in the EEA)
\+ dOS£G
(debt sales to the overseas sector)
\+ dOF$
(official foreign currency borrowing) (2)

The division of the sources of finance corresponds closely to that in *FS* Table 2.6.

(iii) The counterparts to £M3

The final identity used is that £M3 is defined as notes and coin in circulation with the non-bank private sector (PRVNAC) plus sterling denominated private sector deposits with the UK monetary sector:

£M3 = PRVNAC + PRV£D
and
d£M3 = dPRVNAC + dPRV£D (3)

The banks' balance sheet identity (1a) can be rearranged so that deposits included in £M3 equal total bank assets less those liabilities not included in the definition of £M3

dPRV£D = d(PUB£L + PUB$L + PRV£L + PRV$L + OS£L + OS$L)

-d(PUB£D + PUB$D + PRV$D + OS£D + OS$D + NNDL) (1b)

Identity (1b) can then be substituted into identity (3) so that the change in £M3 equals the change in notes and coin held by the non-bank private sector plus total bank assets less bank liabilities not included in the definition of £M3. This yields:

d£M3 =

dPRVNAC

+ d(PUB£L + PUB$L + PRV£L + PRV$L + OS£L + OS$L)

- d(PUB£D + PUB$D + PRV$D + OS£D + OS$D + NNDL) (3a)

The public sector financing identity (2) can then be rearranged so that bank lending to the sector in sterling equals the PSBR less its other financing components:

dPUB£L = PSBR-dPRV£G + dIDCB - dOS£G - dPRVNAC + dRES - dOF$
-dPUB$L + dPUB£D + dPUB$D (2a)

This provides a natural interpretation of the public sector financing identity since in many ways the banking sector provides the residual form of finance to the public sector.

Since bank lending to the public sector can be expressed in terms of the PSBR and its other financing components, identity (2a) can be substituted into identity (3a) giving:

d£M3 =
(change in £M3)
PSBR
(public sector borrowing requirement)
-dPRV£G
(sales of public sector debt to the non-bank private sector)
+ d(PRV£L + IDCB)
(bank lending in sterling to UK residents including Issue Department purchases of commercial bills)
+ d(OS£L - OS£D)
(sterling deposits from, net of loans to, overseas (increase-))
+ d(PRV$L - PRV$D + OS$L - OS$D)
(banks' net foreign currency deposit liabilities (increase-))
+ d(RES - OF$ - OS£G)
(external finance of the public sector (increase -))
- dNNDL
(net non-deposit liabilities) (3b)

Three modifications can be made to identity (3b) so that it corresponds more closely to the format of *BEQB* Table 11.3. First, we can express the PSBR as:

PSBR = CGBR
+ LABR - on-lending from central government
+ PCBR - on-lending from central government
= CGBR + other public sector contribution (OPSC) (4)

where:

CGBR = central government borrowing requirement
(which includes borrowing required to finance CG on-lending to local authorities (LAs) and public corporations (PCs).
LABR = LAs borrowing requirement
PCBR = PCs borrowing requirement

It follows from identity (4) that CGBR + OPSC can be substituted for PSBR in identity (3b). In *BEQB* Table 11.3, CG and OPS debt sales are reported separately (columns 3 and 4). However, the OPS only reports its debt sales on a calendar quarterly basis, and only the net effect of the other public sector on the money supply (OPSC - debt sales) can be identified from the monthly banking returns. The CGBR + OPSC - OPS debt sales (columns 1, 2 and 3) is sometimes referred to as the amended PSBR.

Second, sterling deposits from, net of loans to, overseas can be disaggregated. In *BEQB* Table 11.3, claims on liabilities to banks overseas are distinguished from those relating to other non-residents and three separate items are distinguished:

i) sterling deposits from, net of market loans to, banks abroad (increase -);
ii) other overseas sterling deposits (increase -);
iii) other sterling lending to overseas sector.

Third, net non-deposit liabilities can be split into sterling and foreign currency components. This change was introduced in the June 1985 *BEQB*. As foreign currency capital issues by banks are unlikely to be financed to a large extent by a rundown of UK residents' sterling deposits, the impact on £M3 is likely to be small. Such issues are likely to be financed by a rundown of foreign currency deposits. Thus, if foreign currency capital issues are classified along with sterling issues in NNDLs, an issue of foreign currency capital is likely to involve a rise in NNDLs (reducing £M3 growth) as well as a reduction in foreign currency deposits (raising the external influences on £M3 growth). The new approach of grouping foreign currency net non-deposit liabilities with the other external and foreign currency counterparts avoids such movements in the counterparts and is likely to aid interpretation.

Making these three changes to identity (3b) gives the familiar expression of the counterparts to £M3 identity reported in *BEQB* Table 11.3 and the Bank of England's monthly *Banking Statistics* Press Release. By way of illustration, Table 3.10 gives recent data. The counterparts of £M3 identity does not provide any information about the causes of money supply growth. The relationship between changes in £M3 and its counterparts is merely a statistical artifact consequent upon the definition of £M3 and various balance sheet identities. Nevertheless, *BEQB* Table 11.3 can be used as a framework for analysing monetary developments if it is used in conjunction with knowledge about the factors affecting each component and the relationship between them.

Table 3.10: Public Sector Borrowing Requirement, and other counterparts to changes in money stock

Month ended	Domestic counterparts					External and foreign currency counterparts						Sterling net non deposit liabilities (NNDL£) (inc-)	Money stock £M3
	Public Sector Borrowing Requirement (PSBR)	Purchases of public sector debt by UK private sector (dPRV£G)		Sterling lending to UK private sector plus issue Dept's holdings of commercial bills (d(PRV£L+IDCB))	Sub-total of cols 1-5	Sterling deposits from, net of loans to, overseas (d(OS£L-OS£D)) (increase-)			Banks' net foreign currency liabilities (d(PRV$L-PRV$D+OS$L-OS$D-NNDL$)) (increase-)	External finance of the public sector (d(RES-OF$-OS£G)) (increase-)	Sub-total of cols 7-11		
	Central Government Borrowing Requirement (CGBR)	Other public sector contribution (OPSC) / Other public sector	Central Government debt			Sterling deposits from, net of market loans to, banks abroad (inc-)	Other overseas sterling deposits (inc-)	Other sterling lending to o'seas sector					
	1	2–3	4	5	6	7	8	9	10	11	12	13	14
1984													
Jul 18	-42	-279	-804	1,184	59	-135	-137	122	-139	-311	-600	505	-36
Aug 15	924	288	-1,554	162	-180	144	-115	-174	264	194	313	411	544
Sep 19	1,180	141	-842	973	1,452	-547	111	826	-362	-588	-560	167	1,059
Oct 17	293	50	-1,457	3,136	2,022	-253	-637	382	75	135	-298	-1,122	602
Nov 21	1,994	478	-1,538	1,503	2,437	-269	-354	699	174	-24	226	78	2,741
Dec 12	773	-79	-531	385	548	177	-95	268	-333	125	142	-345	345
1985													
Jan 16	-2,005	295	-974	3,012	328	602	-487	356	-383	-413	-325	-164	-161
Feb 20	-310	93	-1,560	1,351	-426	-270	-57	202	204	-659	-580	669	-337
Mar 20	361	56	-1,146	1,839	1,110	-1,711	-25	163	1,774	-216	-15	-724	371
Apr 17	2,783	354	-1,384	2,831	4,584	375	-286	251	741	-83	998	-1,209	4,373
May 15	496	66	-699	865	728	301	-68	269	-468	-130	-96	-388	244
Jun 19	2,642	-433	-224	760	2,745	317	-256	-275	1,230	-463	553	-331	2,967
Jul 17	-1,158	-417	-421	3,106	1,110	116	-360	-405	348	-409	-710	-468	-68

(Corresponds with Table A in the Bank of England's monthly *Banking Statistics* Press Release and Table 11.3 in *BEQB*)

In the next two sections, we discuss the factors influencing the domestic and external counterparts.

(iv) The domestic counterparts

Domestic counterparts and DCE

In *BEQB* Table 11.3, the domestic counterparts are distinguished from the external and foreign currency counterparts and net non-deposit liabilities. The domestic counterparts consist of the first three elements of equation (3b), i.e. the PSBR minus debt sales to the UK private sector plus bank lending in sterling to the UK private sector. Until June 1983, the Bank also published data for domestic credit expansion (DCE) defined as the sum of the domestic counterparts plus sterling lending to overseas residents (OS£L). This definition of DCE was considered appropriate when sterling lending to overseas was used primarily to purchase UK exports, and therefore had a similar effect on the domestic economy as direct lending to the UK exporter. Following the abolition of exchange controls (in October 1979) and the final removal of the corset (in June 1980) the reasons for sterling lending overseas probably changed markedly. First, much of the growth of sterling lending to overseas banks during the early 1980s reflected an international expansion of the London interbank market, with the effect of the increased lending on £M3 often largely offset by higher sterling deposits placed by banks overseas with banks in the UK. Secondly, sterling lending to non-banks was increasingly used to finance trade between third countries, which again does not directly affect the UK economy. These considerations led to the change in the presentation of the external influences on money in 1981, with sterling lending to overseas residents included in the external rather than the domestic counterparts, and to less emphasis being placed on DCE.

The International Monetary Fund's preferred definition of DCE has, however, always excluded overseas sterling lending (although it includes foreign currency lending to the private sector and excludes the other public sector contribution) and clearly it would have been possible to redefine DCE without reducing the emphasis placed on it.

The interpretation of movements in DCE is, however, simpler under a fixed rather than a floating exchange rate regime. Under a fixed rate system, excessive DCE growth would manifest itself partly in the form of a deterioration of the balance of payments which would be financed by running down the official reserves. A fall in the reserves, however, would produce a contractionary effect on broad money which may then appear to be developing satisfactorily. It was argued that in such circumstances it was more appropriate to look at DCE rather than broad monetary growth as an indicator of the stance of financial policies.

Furthermore, changes in international portfolio preferences will be important in assessing divergent movements between DCE and broad monetary growth in a country whose residents hold large amounts of foreign currency and whose currency is held in substantial amounts by non-residents (as is the case with the UK).

Bank lending to the private sector

In recent years, bank lending to the non-bank private sector has been the most important counterpart to the change in £M3, in the sense that variations in £M3 are due largely to variations in bank lending. For this reason, it is the most closely watched of all the counterparts to £M3 growth. As we stated in the introduction to this chapter, banks now predominantly liability manage: that is, they meet the demands for credit made on them and then bid for deposits in order to finance that demand. Thus explanation and forecasting of the demand for credit takes on particular importance in the explanation and forecasting of £M3. The authorities have, however, been notably unsuccessful in explaining the changes in bank lending which have occurred, witness Goodhart[1]:

> Indeed, we [the Bank of England] have not generally been able either to forecast in advance, or even to explain in retrospect, the fluctuations in bank lending to the private sector, the explosion in 1971-3, the period of quiescence 1974-7, the extended surge 1978-82.

Moreover, econometric studies on the demand for credit have generally found that there is only a relatively weak effect of interest rates on demand: thus *control* of credit demand may be difficult. Indeed, a number of studies have found that there is no reduction in the demand for bank credit as interest rates rise; in those studies where an influence has been found, the reduction in demand has taken an appreciable time to come through.

Certainly, it is unlikely that any appreciable reduction will occur within six months. One reason for this is that a rise in interest rates, by raising the 'interest bill' acts to raise the demand for credit in the short run (a comprehensive survey of econometric work on the demand for credit is presented as Appendix 2 to Chapter IV in Goodhart[1]).

The conclusion for the authorities is that, with bank lending the most important counterpart to £M3 growth, and with that counterpart largely insensitive to interest rates in the short run, short term control of £M3 by changing interest rates is largely implausible (this conclusion is underscored by the fact that other counterparts may also respond in an unhelpful manner in the short run — see later).

Direct controls on bank lending are an alternative way of moderating the growth of credit. No form of direct control is, however, used at present and it is highly unlikely that any will be implemented in the near future. The last form of direct control used on the banking system was the 'corset': it is worthwhile, at this point, to examine the reasons for its downfall.

The scheme imposed penalties on banks whose interest bearing eligible liabilities (IBELs, broadly their interest bearing sterling deposits) grew faster than a prescribed rate. The penalties were progressive, being greater the larger the extent of overshoot of the prescribed growth. The scheme was used on three separate occasions: from December 1973 to February 1975; from November 1976 to August 1977; and from June 1978 to June 1980. In acting to restrain the growth of interest bearing sterling deposits, the scheme recognised the movement to liability management by the banking sector. It was largely effective in controlling the growth of deposits.

The UK banking sector responded to the controls, however, by diverting business through other channels. Specifically, two types of disintermediation of the banking sector occurred. First, the use of acceptance facilities became more popular: with this, a bank would agree to accept (i.e. guarantee) bills issued by a customer. These could then be sold to non-banks — the bank's guarantee making them highly marketable — and would not appear on the accepting bank's balance sheet: they were thus excluded from IBELs. The growth of holdings of such bank bills was well known and was referred to as the 'bill leak'. Second, after the abolition of exchange controls in October 1979, UK residents were able freely to deposit with, and borrow from, banks overseas. This brought the possibility of channelling any excess growth of IBELs through offshore subsidiaries of UK banks (which were outside the controlled sector). In both cases, the UK banking sector no longer appeared as the intermediary — disintermediation occurred — but the effect was purely 'cosmetic' in the sense that overall credit and liquidity in the economy were broadly unaffected. Measures could have been taken to control both problems — indeed, the Governor of the Bank requested that banks should not avoid the controls by using offshore subsidiaries — but they risked further disintermediation which was less likely to be observed and controlled by the authorities.

At that time the experience of the 'secondary banking crisis' was still fresh in the minds of the authorities. During the 1960s when direct controls on bank lending were in force, much of the frustrated business passed to a secondary banking sector, largely outside the supervision of the authorities. When controls were removed in 1971, much of the diverted business was channelled back through the primary banks, leading to a collapse of confidence in the secondary banks and the launch of the Bank's 'lifeboat'. A re-run of that episode was clearly unwanted.

In the light of these problems, the 'corset' was taken off in June 1980. The bill leak contracted sharply as the banking sector reintermediated business. £M3 grew sharply, which was an acute embarrassment for the government who had recently recast monetary control in the new mould of their Medium Term Financial Strategy.

We are, thus, now in the position where the authorities are (i) unwilling to use any form of direct control over the growth of banking business and (ii) not convinced that higher interest rates can exert any significant downward pressure on credit demand and monetary growth in the short term. In this environment, short term control of £M3 has come to rely heavily on management of the government's funding programme. Before turning to that, we discuss a factor which has been important in influencing the growth of bank lending — 'round-tripping'.

Round-tripping

Round-tripping refers to the practice of borrowing in one market and depositing the proceeds in another so as to yield a profit. It can act to expand both measured bank lending to the private sector and £M3. There are two main types of round tripping which occur. The first type involves borrowing at a base rate related interest rate (say base rate plus 1% for good corporate customers) and depositing the proceeds in the money market at a higher rate. Such possibilities arise if the banks are slow to adjust their base rates in response to movements in market rates. The main problem for the 'round-tripper' is that if base rates change, the profitability of the process can be eliminated: because of this, such round-tripping probably involves relatively short term money market deposits (say, seven day) in order to reduce exposure to base rate movements. If such round-tripping occurs over the monthly make-up day for the banking statistics, both bank lending and £M3 will be inflated. Clearly, however, if it both occurs and unwinds within the banking month, no rise in the banking statistics will occur. With the banks now changing their base rates more speedily in response to market movements in interest rates, the scope for such round-tripping has been reduced.

The second, and much more widespread, type of round-tripping is between bills and wholesale deposits. With this, a company can draw a bill and have it accepted by a bank. The bill can then be discounted at one of the discount houses. At certain times the proceeds from discounting the bill (even after allowing for the acceptance commission payable to the bank) may be reinvested in the money market at a profit. It is quite straightforward to monitor the profitability of such a series of transactions: Figure 3.1, for example, shows an estimate of the profitability for the period January to March 1985. It is assumed that a bill is drawn, accepted by a bank at a commission of ¼% and the proceeds redeposited in the interbank market. Appropriate allowance is made for bid/offer spreads (and it should be remembered that bill rates are quoted as discounts and interbank rates as yields). The calculations for Figure 3.1 are performed for one month instruments but round-tripping opportunities can equally well exist at other maturities. As can be seen from the chart, the profitability of such round-tripping was as high as £1,000 on a £1m bill at certain times during the period. Indeed, this may well understate the margin as commission rates can be lower and bid/offer spreads finer than those quoted rates which are used.

The first quarter of the year is generally the time at which such round-tripping is most common: that is the period of the bulk of corporate tax payments and consequently the time when money market liquidity is lowest. As explained in Chapter 6, this can act to keep money market interest rates high: if, at the same time, the Bank continues to purchase bills at unchanged rates, it may encourage bill round-tripping opportunities.

It should be noted that with this type of round-tripping, the profitability is assured at the time the transactions are made; there is no risk of a movement in market rates eliminating the profitability of such round tripping (as is the case with base rate related round-tripping). The indications are that bill round-tripping of this type occurs most commonly at maturities of one and three months. In both cases both bank lending and £M3 growth would be inflated over the make-up day following the transaction; and the subsequent 'unwinding' of the round-tripping would depress bank lending and £M3 in later months.

Assessment of the precise extent to which such round tripping takes place is problematical. One particular problem is that an increase in the issuance of bills (which some may take as evidence of the occurrrence of bill round-tripping) may well reflect just the switch to bill finance from other

Figure 3.1: Profitability of bill round-tripping, Jan-March 1985*

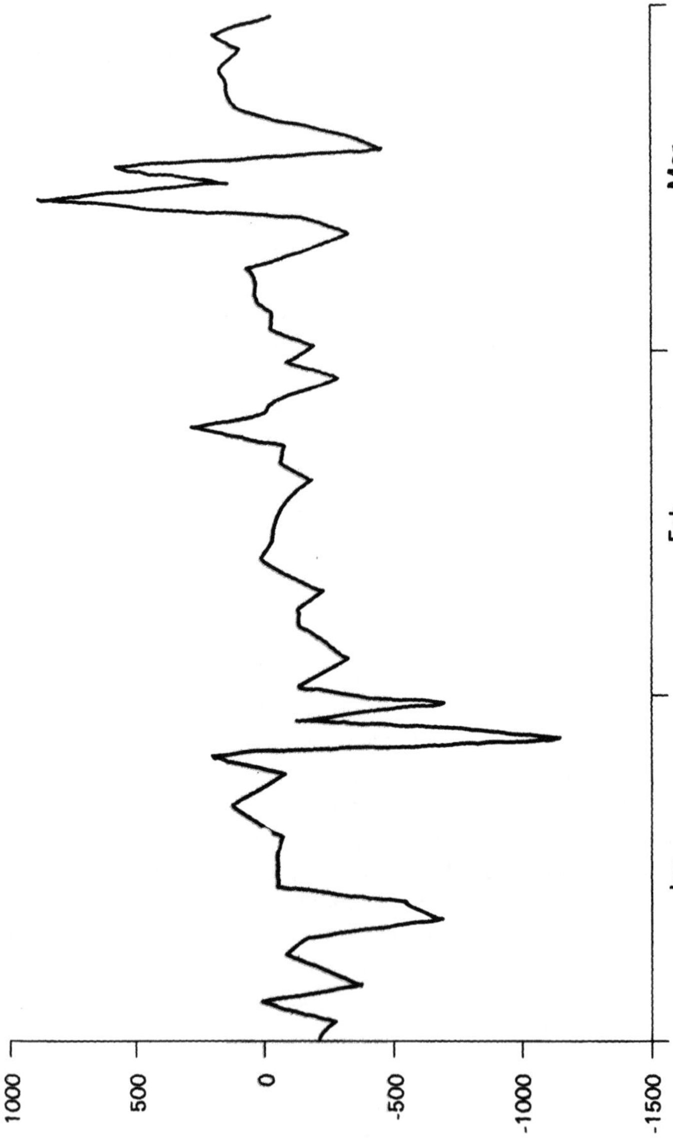

* The chart shows the profit, in £, of drawing a one month bill of face value £1m and reinvesting the proceeds in the interbank market.

forms of borrowing (say, a base rate related overdraft): this has been termed *soft arbitrage* and will not lead to a rise in bank lending or £M3. Only where the proceeds from the issue of the bill are deposited in the money market will *hard arbitrage*, and inflation of bank lending and £M3, occur.

Overfunding

Throughout most of the period of monetary targetting in the UK, the main expansionary stimulus has come from bank lending to the private sector. In order to mitigate the effects of this on £M3, the authorities have, from time to time, chosen to overfund the PSBR. Overfunding occurs when UK non-bank residents' net purchases of public sector debt exceed the PSBR (alternative definitions are occasionally used). Table 3.11 shows the actual growth in £M3, bank lending and the extent of overfunding from 1977/78 to 1984/85. Overfunding occurred in 1977/78, 1981/82, 1983/84 and 1984/85: over the entire period debt sales exceeded the PSBR by £5½ billion. The increase in bank lending to the UK private sector over the same period was £92 billion. An important consequence of overfunding has been

Table 3.11: £M3 and overfunding, 1977/78 to 1984/85

£ billions	77/78	78/79	79/80	80/81	81/82	82/83	83/84	84/85
Growth in £M3	6.2	5.3	6.4	10.3	9.7	9.8	7.6	12.0
Bank lending to UK private sector	3.7	6.3	9.3	9.2	14.9	14.4	15.4	18.8
PSBR	5.5	9.2	9.9	12.7	8.6	8.9	9.8	10.1
UK non-bank residents' net purchases of public sector debt	6.9	8.5	9.2	10.8	11.3	8.4	12.6	12.4
Overfunding (underfunding -)	1.4	-0.7	-0.7	-1.9	2.7	-0.4	2.8	2.3

the shortage of liquidity created in the money market. This arises as net payments to the Exchequer accounts at the Bank from the rest of the banking system (due to central government expenditure being smaller than central government receipts from taxation and the sale of gilts) drain money market liquidity. The Bank then relieves this shortage, normally by purchasing bills from the discount houses. Until recently, the discount houses held plentiful stocks of Treasury bills and the Bank could purchase these from the houses in order to relieve the shortage. But more recently, with stocks of Treasury bills held by the houses at a low level, the offsetting money market operations have been largely in terms of purchases of commercial bills.

It should be noted that the link between overfunding, money market shortages and the Bank's purchases of bills is not a totally straightforward one. First, overfunding relates to the total public sector whereas it is only the position of the central government which influences money market liquidity. Second, other factors can be an important influence on the money market shortage (including changes in the note circulation, government debt sales to the banks and overseas). Third, the effect of overfunding on £M3 growth is normally defined in seasonally adjusted terms, whereas it is non-seasonally adjusted cash flows which impact on the money market shortage (all these factors are discussed in detail in Chapter 6).

Despite these caveats, overfunding has been an important influence on the Bank's need to purchase commercial bills in recent years. The cumulative effects of money market shortages have led to a substantial accumulation of commercial bills by the Bank: this has come to be termed the 'bill mountain'. In early 1985 the mountain was widely thought to have been of the order of £15bn (reasonable estimates of its size can be gleaned from the weekly *Bank Return*). These bills can be held by either the Bank's Issue Department or Banking Department. Issue Department's holdings of commercial bills are included in the counterpart 'bank lending to the private sector' (as shown earlier). This does not, however, imply that the impact of overfunding on the growth of £M3 is in some way 'neutralised', as suggested by some commentators. Issue Department buys bills from the discount houses; as the houses are included in the monetary sector, the transaction involves their lending to the private sector falling, and Issue Department's lending rising by the same amount. If Banking Department buys the bills then, as it is part of the monetary sector, a transfer of ownership of bills within the sector occurs and again the total of bank lending as a counterpart to £M3 is unaffected.

With the Bank acquiring bills on such a large scale it is understandable that questions about the suitability of this technique of monetary management have been raised. The process can be viewed as the Bank (acting as the agent of the government) lending to the private sector, borrowing in the gilt market in order to be able to do so. As Fforde[2] commented, the process of overfunding 'must in the end raise questions about the politico-economic "interface" between the central government and the corporate sector'.

The need to overfund would be reduced if the corporate sector itself borrowed in the capital markets. The Bank would then no longer need to act as an intermediary. The Bank has taken measures in order to stimulate this development. First, it aimed to reduce the amount of funding at the long end of the gilt market in order to relieve pressure on long term interest rates and thus encourage the corporate sector to borrow directly in this market. The policy appeared to change the shape of the yield curve (see Chapter 8) but overseas sovereign borrowers, rather than UK corporates, proved to be the only very active participants in the long bond market as a result. Second, measures were taken in the 1985 Finance Act to allow companies to issue short corporate bonds. As yet it is too early to say whether this will help reduce corporate demand for bank credit but the preliminary indications are encouraging.

(v) The external counterparts

Using the modifications to identity (3b) discussed above, the external and foreign currency counterparts (XFCC) can be expressed as:

XFCC =
(*external and foreign currency counterparts*)

- dOS£D + dOS£L (banks)
(*sterling deposits from, net of loans to, banks abroad* (*increase* -))

- dOS£D (non banks)
(*other overseas sterling deposits* (*increase* -))

+ dOS£L (non banks)
(*other sterling lending to overseas sector*)

+ dPRV$L - dPRV$D + dOS$L -dOS$D
(*banks' net foreign currency deposit liabilities* (*increase* -))

+ dRES - dOF$ - dOS£G
(*external finance of the public sector* (*increase* -)) (5)

The expressions on the right hand side refer to the expressions used in the counterparts Table 11.3 in the *BEQB* (we have adopted, because of data availability for Table 3.12 below, the 'old' split between the externals and net non-deposit liabilities, i.e. the one in which foreign currency capital flows are included in NNDLs and not the externals).

The split of OS£D (overseas sector deposits in sterling with UK banks) and OS£L (lending by UK banks in sterling to overseas sector) between 'banks' and 'non-banks' was introduced in December 1981. The abolition of exchange controls (in 1979) and the final withdrawal of the 'corset' in June 1980, facilitated the growth of the eurosterling market and its greater integration with the London interbank market. As a result, both banks' sterling lending to, and deposits from, overseas have been inflated, although the net effect has been small. The new classification enables the extent of the growth due to interbank business to be separated from that due to other business.

The system of banks' balance sheet reporting is not exactly consistent with the balance of payments accounts. However, an accounting identity linkage can be established between the balance of payments and the external and foreign currency counterparts of £M3. The balance of payments identity can be expressed as follows:

$$CB+ETP+ETG+d(OS£D-OS£L)+dOS£G+d(OS\$D-OS\$L)-dRES+dOF\$ = 0 \quad (6)$$

where:

CB = *current balance*

ETP = *private sector external capital transactions*

ETG = *public sector external capital transactions contributing to, as distinct from financing, the PSBR*

d (OS£D - OS£L) = *change in banks' net sterling liabilities to overseas sector*

d OS£G = *change in overseas sectors' holdings of British government debt*

d(OS$D-OS$L) = *change in banks' net foreign currency liabilities to overseas sector*

- dRES + dOF$ = *change in international reserves in the Exchange Equalisation Account, net of official foreign currency borrowing*

that is: a (public and private) balance of payments current and capital account imbalance must be equal to, and of opposite sign to, its financing counterparts. For example, a balance of payments surplus on current and capital account can be financed by: (i) a rundown of overseas residents' (net) sterling or foreign currency deposits; (ii) a rundown of overseas residents' holdings of gilts; or (iii) (largely under a fixed exchange rate regime) an increase in foreign currency reserves (net of official foreign currency borrowing). Rearranging equation (5) and substituting into equation (6) yields:

XFCC = CB + ETP + ETG + dPRV$L - dPRV$D

This corresponds to the presentation of the relationship between the external and foreign currency counterparts and the balance of payments given in *FS* Table 11.6. By way of illustration, recent data are given in Table 3.12.

Table 3.12: Relationship between external and foreign currency counterparts and the balance of payments

	XFCC	CB	ETP	ETG	dPRV$L	dPRV$D	Residual (including balancing item)
1977	3948	-128	970	-312	1215	-758	2961
1978	200	972	-2205	-40	1020	-1334	1787
1979	-3058	-736	-2941	229	902	-779	267
1980	-882	3100	-3527	182	1278	-1872	-43
1981	157	6528	-6370	409	2792	-2417	-785
1982	-1901	4663	-6042	570	1741	-820	-2013
1983	-3297	3168	-5682	-534	1411	-4839	3179
1984	-3582	935	-7840	-297	4735	-5463	4348

Corresponds to Table 11.6 in FS.

As far as the analysis of monthly changes in the external and foreign currency counterparts is concerned this framework is, for several reasons, of only limited use. First, banking monthly data for the balance of payments data are not available. Second, even if such data were available they are particularly prone to revision. Third, the residual item (incorporating the balance of payments balancing item in Table 3.12) can be particularly large in relation to the other flows.

During a particular period there may be information available in relation to one of the individual components of the external and foreign currency counterparts and the question of the influence of this on £M3 often arises. Taking a particular example, it may be known that purchases of gilts by overseas residents have been strong during a certain period (for example, this happened in the first half of 1985). Such sales — represented as dOS£G in equation (5) above — will, other things being equal, reduce £M3. Such a simple analysis may, however, prove misleading: particularly with the external and foreign currency counterparts, there may be associated transactions which offset, or even reverse, the effect of the transaction on £M3. Taking the example of gilt sales to overseas we consider below several ways in which they may be financed and the consequences for £M3.

First, consider the example in which purchases of gilts from central government are financed by a rundown of sterling deposits with the UK monetary sector. In this case, overseas sterling deposits fall (an expansionary influence on £M3 growth), matching the contractionary influence from the gilt sale and £M3 is unchanged. Example 1 in Table 3.13 sets out the transactions (the same effect on £M3 results if the gilt purchase is financed by borrowing in sterling from the UK monetary sector).

More likely, however, the purchase of gilts will reflect a general move into sterling assets by the overseas sector. Consider a second example, therefore, in which the overseas sector holds foreign currency deposits (again with the UK monetary sector) and switches these into sterling. Foreign currency deposits with the UK monetary sector fall, an expansionary influence on £M3, but the increase in overseas sterling deposits is contractionary to the same extent, leaving the overall effect on £M3 again zero. Examining the components of £M3, rather than its counterparts, the conclusion is arrived at more simply: the UK non-bank private sector's sterling deposits are unchanged by the sequence of transactions. If, as above, these sterling deposits are then used to buy gilts from central government, £M3 is unchanged. The sequence of the four transactions is set out as Example 2 in Table 3.13.

A third example involves an overseas resident converting a foreign currency deposit with a bank outside the UK monetary sector into sterling and then placing the funds on deposit with the UK monetary sector. The first round effect of this is a reduction in £M3 (see Example 3). If these deposits are then used to purchase gilts from central government, we again have the sequence of transactions as set out in Example 1; the overall effect is that £M3 falls.

If the gilts were bought from the UK non-bank private sector or the UK monetary sector and not central government, rather different effects on £M3 would occur. In the first case, £M3 is likely to rise. Overseas residents' sterling deposits fall as they use these deposits to purchase gilts from the UK non-bank private sector: that sector's deposits rise, increasing £M3.

Table 3.13: Examples of the influence of overseas purchases of gilts on £M3

	Effect on £M3
Example 1:	
Overseas £ deposits fall	+100
Overseas purchase of gilts from CG	-100
Total effect	0
Example 2:	
Overseas f/c deposits fall	+100
Overseas £ deposits rise	-100
Overseas £ deposits fall	+100
Overseas purchase of gilts from CG	-100
Total effect	0
Example 3:	
Overseas £ deposits rise	-100
Overseas £ deposits fall	+100
Overseas purchase of gilts from CG	-100
Total effect	-100
Example 4:	
Overseas £ deposits fall	+100
Overseas purchase of gilts from NBPS	-100
Sale of gilts by NBPS	+100
Total effect	+100
Example 5:	
Overseas £ deposits fall	+100
Overseas purchase of gilts from UK banks	-100
Total effect	0

The effect of the transactions on the £M3 counterparts is set out as Example 4 in the table. Purchases of gilts by the overseas sector from the UK monetary sector would leave £M3 unchanged (Example 5).

Implications of foreign exchange intervention for £M3

Some advocates of monetary targets believe that a freely floating exchange rate is a necessary concomitant of meeting monetary targets. Moreover, in an open economy such as the UK, the main channel by which monetary policy works may be via the exchange rate. The 'international monetarist' school has argued that if the supply of money in the UK is allowed to grow faster than the demand for money, UK residents will seek to run down their sterling balances. In an open economy one of the quickest and easiest ways for UK residents to reduce their money balances is to purchase foreign currencies either to hold on deposit, or to purchase imports, overseas equities or bonds. As a result the sterling exchange rate may fall, the sterling price of imports may rise, UK nominal earnings may rise and, therefore, the general price level may rise. Thus, control of domestic credit may, according to this view, facilitate the control of inflation.

A slightly different view of the interaction between money and prices via the exchange rate leads to broadly similar conclusions. In order to meet a monetary target the authorities may have to raise short term sterling interest rates. If the uncovered interest rate differential moves in favour of sterling and the exchange rate is not expected to decline, the demand for sterling may rise and consequently the spot exchange rate may appreciate. The high exchange rate may tend to moderate rises in the sterling price of imports and substitutes: the decline in the rate of growth of prices may retard the rate of growth of earnings throughout the economy and hence the general level of prices. This view of the transmission mechanism from money to prices differs from the international monetarist view because, it is claimed, the authorities are able to induce discretionary changes in domestic interest rates. In the international monetarist model the authorities cannot vary sterling interest rates at their discretion because they are constrained by the rates set in international capital markets.

Whatever the exact nature of the transmission mechanism, if causality runs from the exchange rate to the price level, it might be argued that the authorities should seek to keep the exchange rate within a predetermined band, rather than adhere to a monetary target. If inflation rates exceed what are considered to be desirable for the UK, an appreciating target could be set. If causality runs from the price level to the exchange rate, it may be appropriate for the authorities to accommodate price rises by allowing the nominal exchange rate to depreciate, thereby keeping to a real exchange rate target.

Non-intervention by the EEA does not necessarily preclude the effect of external factors on £M3. If non-bank UK residents switch out of sterling and this switch is unwound by the UK banks rather than by non-residents (i.e. UK banks' net foreign currency liabilities rise), £M3 will decline. Conversely attempts to meet a (nominal) exchange rate target, such as in the period up to October 1977, may not initially lead to loss of control of £M3. The positive effect of rises in international reserves in the EEA on £M3 may be offset by rises in overseas sterling deposits and overseas purchases of gilts. If interest rates are expected to decline in order to keep (the uncovered interest rate differential and therefore) the sterling exchange rate down, residents and non-residents may be more willing to buy gilts, and monetary control may be assisted. The inflow may enable the banks to lower their sterling certificate of deposit and ordinary deposit rates, thereby encouraging some UK residents to reduce their sterling balances.

However, falls in interest rates may stimulate (with a lag) the demand for credit and hence increase the stock of £M3. Thus, in the medium term, if not in the short run, an independent target for the exchange rate is likely to be incompatible with a target for £M3. Even in the short run it may not be possible to 'sterilise' all inflows: a commitment to an exchange rate target, particularly one which is expected to be exceeded, may encourage UK residents (perhaps companies) to switch foreign currency into sterling balances in the UK, thereby raising £M3. The adoption of dual £M3 and exchange rate targets, which were 'flexible' in the sense that both could be rebased every six months, might lead to perverse fluctuations in the money supply and interest rates. If sterling was expected to rise or decline, but the authorities only allowed the rate to adjust every six months, speculators could take positions against the authorities. The EEA intervention might have to be extremely large, with the resultant consequences for £M3, and the cost of intervention might be considerable.

(vi) Net non-deposit liabilities (NNDLs)

Banks' non-deposit liabilities consist mainly of their capital and reserves. When various assets — predominantly plant, equipment and leased assets — are deducted, we arrive at the total for *net* non-deposit liabilities (NNDLs).

NNDLs are defined as the residual item in a bank's balance sheet, being the difference between the total balance sheet size and deposits. For the consolidated balance sheet of the monetary sector, any error on consolidation (or 'interbank difference', see page 31) is included in NNDLs.

Retention of profits and issue of equity or bonds are the main ways in which the monetary sector can strengthen its capital base. An increase in (undistributed) profits will expand the liability side of the monetary sector's balance sheet. In this way, an increase in profits can act as the counterpart to an increase in lending and a substitute for deposit creation. Profits arising from the revaluation of foreign currency business are also included in NNDLs. As discussed in the earlier example, if the monetary sector has net foreign currency liabilities, any rise in the value of sterling against other currencies will bring a profit and a rise in NNDLs.

In the monthly data for the counterparts, NNDLs can be very volatile, in large part because they include consolidation error. They are generally very difficult to forecast in advance. Broadly, however, higher interest rates may help bank profitability (to the extent that they increase the profit banks make on their non-interest bearing deposits, the so-called 'endowment effect') and help to reduce monetary growth.

(vii) Seasonal adjustment of £M3

The Bank attempts to remove systematic fluctuations in £M3 and its counterparts which occur within a year. In principle the seasonally adjusted series should retain systematic fluctuations which occur less frequently than once a year (trend) and random fluctuations (noise). A number of programmes are available which use moving average filtering methods to remove seasonal frequencies. The Central Statistical Office uses a modified version of the X-11 programme, which was originally devised for the Department of Commerce in the United States. The Bank of England uses a programme known as SADJMO which is similar in principle, but was devised within the Bank. Another method called 'signal extraction' fits a model to the data, after identifying 'outliers' (unusually large or small observations) and decomposes the series into trend, seasonal and random components. The use of different seasonal adjustment programmes is of little substantive importance, although it can pose problems for econometric analysis.

Unfortunately the system of monthly banks' balance sheet reporting, and the importance of public sector transactions as a source of seasonality in the money supply presents a number of difficulties which complicate the problem of seasonally adjusting money. The central government's receipts and payments follow a pre-determined pattern, although this can be changed substantially.

The banks submit balance sheets for close of business on the third Wednesday of the month (second Wednesday in December). This is arguably preferable to the last working day of the calendar month because transit items are substantial at that time, and an adjustment would have to be made for the day of the week. However, as a result of third Wednesday reporting three factors tend to have an important impact on the seasonal pattern of the figures, which cannot be picked up with conventional seasonal adjustment techniques:

(a) the third Wednesday falls between the 15th and 21st of the month and therefore make-up day can occur before or after the monthly PAYE payments. If make-up day occurs after the 19th, bank lending will tend to be higher and deposits will tend to be lower;
(b) the change over the banking month will vary depending on whether there are four or five weeks in the month;
(c) quarterly interest debiting and crediting by banks will affect bank lending and deposits in the banking months in which it occurs.

No moving average seasonal adjustment model can allow for these calendar effects, and therefore the series is prior adjusted for the anticipated effects of these factors before being put through the seasonal adjustment programme.

Prior adjustments are also made for changes in the timing of central government transactions: from time to time the seasonal pattern of the CGBR (and therefore £M3) changes abruptly because of timing changes in receipts and payments. A moving average model would only incorporate these changes fully after three or more years. As a result, timing changes are anticipated and a prior adjustment is made before the series is put through the seasonal adjustment programme. After the 'pure' seasonal factor has been estimated using the prior adjusted series, the prior adjustments are added back (post adjustments) so that the published seasonal comprises the 'pure' seasonal plus the prior adjustments. Revisions to the seasonals can arise because of the addition of more recent data, but also because of errors in the prior adjustments. For example, an unanticipated change in the pattern of mainstream corporation tax receipts in the first quarter of 1978 required a change in the seasonals for banking January, February and March.

The published seasonals are balanced so that the sum of the seasonals on the counterparts of £M3 presented in *BEQB* Table 11.3 equals the seasonal on £M3 itself. The seasonals are constrained so that the sum of seasonals on the changes in bank liabilities equals the sum of the seasonals on bank assets. As a result, seasonally adjusted bank liabilities equal seasonally adjusted bank assets. The seasonal on the CGBR is estimated separately and the seasonal on the external and foreign currency finance component of £M3 is constrained to equal the seasonal on the balance of payments (calendar months adjusted to banking months). Thus, information on the seasonal pattern of some of the counterparts of £M3 is used to estimate the total seasonal on £M3 and the seasonals are balanced so that they are consistent.

It is conventional for seasonal adjustments to sum to zero over a year. However, since the seasonal pattern for banking statistics is not recurrent the seasonals cannot sum to zero over more than one twelve month period. Different seasonals could be constructed which centre over the calendar year, the financial year or any other annual period. However, at present seasonals are only published so that they are centred over the banking year (second Wednesday in December to second Wednesday in December). In fact, the seasonals do not necessarily sum to zero over the banking year because of calendar effects on the December make-up days. Even if financial year constrained seasonals were used, interest credited/debited would still be smoothed over calendar half years because interest is credited/debited mainly in January and July. As a result the total seasonal would not sum to zero.

(viii) Counterparts to other measures of broad money

The counterparts to other measures of broad money can be constructed in a similar manner to that described for £M3. The counterparts to PSL2, for example, use the consolidated balance sheet of the banks and the building societies (rather than just the banks) as these are the two types of institution whose liabilities are included in that aggregate. The deposits included in the measurement of PSL2 can then be expressed in terms of the assets of the combined bank and building society sector minus those liabilities not included in the definition of PSL2. The public sector's financing identity can be manipulated in a similar way to that described in section (ii) above. As the non-bank and non-building society private sector's holdings of liquid National Savings and Treasury bills are included in the definition of PSL2, these 'drop out' on construction of the counterparts: their treatment is analogous to that of notes and coin in circulation with the public in the construction of the £M3 counterparts. Similarly, as the building societies are now grouped along with the banks, only sales of government debt to the remaining (i.e. non-bank and non-building society) private sector appear in the counterparts. In place of bank lending to the private sector as a counterpart, both bank and building society lending are counted. Long term bank deposits (included in £M3 but not PSL2) and building society deposits not included in PSL2 enter as a negative counterpart (in a manner analogous to the treatment of foreign currency deposits in the £M3 counterparts)

Notes and References

1. C.A.E. Goodhart, 'Monetary Theory and Practice', (London: Macmillan, 1984), p13.
2. J. S. Fforde, 'Setting Monetary Objectives', *BEQB*, June 1983, p206.

4 Analysing Narrow Money

When Nigel Lawson was appointed Chancellor of the Exchequer in the summer of 1983, immediately after the return of the Conservative party to a second term of office, he embarked upon a review of the Medium Term Financial Strategy (MTFS). The authorities had realised, when they first introduced the MTFS, that 'no single statistical measure of the money supply can be expected fully to encapsulate monetary conditions, and so provide a uniquely correct basis for controlling the complex relationships between monetary growth and prices and nominal incomes'[1]. Certainly, as discussed in the previous chapter, interpretation of £M3 had proved particularly difficult in the early 1980s. In 1982 this was given explicit recognition by the introduction of M1 and PSL2 as supplementary monetary targets. Furthermore, the authorities came to stress more strongly the importance of the examination of a range of financial and economic variables when judging the stance of monetary policy. These included such variables as the exchange rate, asset prices and the behaviour of inflation itself.

The result of Lawson's review seemed, however, to be a movement back from this more pragmatic approach which had characterised the early 1980s to an approach which placed primary reliance on the behaviour of monetary *aggregates*. The aim of policy remained, of course, to continue reducing inflation so as to create the conditions for a sustainable growth of output in the medium term. Lawson aimed to draw a clear distinction between the uses of both 'broad' and 'narrow' measures of money in the assessment of policy. Thus, Lawson in his Mansion House speech on 20th October 1983[2]:

> policy decisions have to be taken with an eye to both the growth of liquidity in the economy — as shown by the broader measures of money — and to the amount of money immediately available for current transactions — as shown by the narrower aggregates.

Formal recognition of this came in the 1984 Budget when two different target ranges were set: one for broad money (£M3) of 6-10% growth during the financial year; and one for narrow money (MO) of 4-8%. During the course of 1984 it became increasingly clear that the behaviour of these two monetary aggregates was of paramount importance in the authorities' thinking — especially in their attitude to the appropriate level of short term interest rates. In particular, the authorities resisted rises in interest rates at times of exchange rate weakness (especially in July and October 1984) on the basis that the behaviour of domestic monetary indicators was satisfactory. Commenting in his Mansion House speech on 18th October 1984[3] on the determination of short term interest rates, Lawson said:

> [the markets] have come to recognise that it is the monetary aggregates that are of central relevance to judging monetary conditions and determining interest rates. That has always been our policy, and it remains so. We take the exchange rate into account when its behaviour suggests that the domestic monetary indicators are giving a false reading.

Furthermore, it was the narrower measures of money (particularly MO) which appeared to be most useful in giving the signals for setting short term interest rates (a subject which Lawson had discussed in his Mansion House speech in the previous year).

When deciding on the switch to MO as the target measure of narrow money, it was thought that it possessed four key attributes:

(i) it was not distorted by changes in the banking system, which rendered the interpretation of other monetary aggregates difficult. Although the behaviour of MO was influenced by changes in the usage of cash, these changes appeared to be reasonably stable and predictable. In the circumstances of the early 1980s it appeared the most appropriate definition of transactions balances to use;

(ii) it appeared to provide leading information about the behaviour of inflation;

(iii) its behaviour was readily explicable by the behaviour of a number of other economic and financial variables — its 'demand was stable';

(iv) it appeared controllable by acceptable variations in short term interest rates.

We examine each of these points in turn in the following sections.

(i) M0 as a measure of transactions balances

One of the most fundamental questions in monetary economics is that of the appropriate definition of money. Figure 2.3, 'Relationships among the Narrow Monetary Aggregates and their Components' shows how different definitions of narrow money are built up. All measures of the money supply include notes and coin in circulation with the public, perhaps the most liquid financial asset. Wider definitions of money add various types of bank deposit and the measures of private sector liquidity (PSL) further include building society deposits. The extent to which the components of the monetary and liquidity aggregates are used for *transactions* purposes rather than *savings* purposes obviously differs. Notes and coins are probably used to only a small extent as savings media whereas building society deposits may be used predominantly for this purpose. If one requires a measure of money used for transactions then some method must be used for splitting the different assets into those used predominantly for this purpose and those which are not. In practice the distinction must, to some extent, prove arbitrary. (Indeed, many have questioned the validity of making a sharp division between the demand for money for transactions purposes[4]). We noted in Chapter 2 that M2 was devised as an aggregate to measure transactions balances. However, a more central role for M2 is ruled out at present by the rather short series of data for it (data are only available from November 1981). There are three alternative measures of narrow money which may be considered suitable: M0; M1; and the non-interest bearing element of M1 (nib M1).

M0 may be considered an appropriate measure of transactions balances as it comprises cash in circulation with the public and in banks' tills and bankers' operational deposits at the Bank which are readily convertible into cash. Nevertheless, bank sight deposits are probably just as liquid as cash. Indeed, in some circumstances (e.g. for large transactions) a cheque drawn on a sight deposit may be more readily acceptable as a means of payment. M1 includes all sight deposits. These can, however, conveniently be split into those which bear interest and those which do not.

There are particular difficulties with the interest bearing element of M1 which render it largely unsuitable for inclusion as a measure of transactions balances. Indeed, this was the primary reason given for dropping M1 as a target aggregate and replacing it with M0. Up until the early 1980s, interest bearing sight deposits accounted for a fairly constant proportion of M1. These were considered to be primarily large overnight balances belonging to companies or financial institutions. In many cases, these balances were likely to be awaiting investment in other instruments (for example, gilt edged stock). It is arguable that, as such, they should be excluded from a transactions measure of money.

In the early 1980s the problems of interpreting this interest bearing element were further compounded by a rapid rise in its share of total sight deposits. According to Johnston[5], the increase came from two sources: wholesale deposits; and retail interest earning sight deposits (until the early 1980s thought to have been only a very small proportion of the total). In both cases a transfer of deposits both from non-interest bearing sight deposits and from more illiquid interest bearing deposits is likely to have taken place. To the extent that the first type of shift occurred, the growth of M1 would not be distorted. However, the shift from non-interest bearing to interest bearing deposits within the total raises the average rate of interest paid on such deposits, and this makes the total less sensitive to movements in the absolute level of interest rates. In these circumstances of structural change, the overall effect of a change in interest rates on the demand for M1 becomes indeterminate. To the extent that the second type of shift occurred (i.e. a shift into sight deposits from interest bearing deposits) the broader measures of money may also have been affected. If funds were attracted into bank deposits and out of other assets, the overall growth of £M3 would have been faster (although some of the shift would have reflected a shift between deposits within £M3).

These problems with M1 and nib M1 were thought seriously to undermine their suitability for targetting. Moreover, Treasury research showed that the demand for nib M1 was quite unstable, consistent with the view that nib M1 was being distorted by the growth of ib M1 With the data restrictions on M2, the choice of narrow monetary aggregate in early 1984 appeared to come down to M0. There was, however, some discussion of the possibility of targetting just notes and coin in circulation with the public rather than M0. Although the levels of bankers' operational deposits and banks' till money are small (see Table 2.4), their changes over the course of a month can be very large and greatly increase the volatility of monthly M0 data compared with notes and coin in circulation with the public. Although the measurement of M0 was changed in order to dampen this volatility (by calculating the monthly data for M0 as the average of the weekly data within the month) the question still remained of why these additional elements were included in the authorities' measure of narrow money. This was especially the case as the econometric properties of notes and coin seemed to be rather more reliable than those of M0. One reason which was advanced was that the inclusion of bankers' operational deposits would ease the path towards a system of monetary base control. Under such a system, these deposits would have an important role to play. (Monetary base control is discussed in more detail in section (iii)). A second reason was the purely presentational one that MO sounded like a monetary aggregate whereas notes and coin in circulation did not.

(ii) MO and inflation

Commenting in his 1983 Mansion House speech, Lawson said:[6]

> it was the surge in the narrow aggregates in 1977 which was followed by the surge in inflation in 1979. And the deceleration in the growth of narrow money in 1979 and 1980 preceded the recent decline in inflation.

This relationship is shown in Figure 4.1. For some time in the UK, the extent to which developments in money provide leading information about the behaviour of inflation has been a subject of heated debate. In part, the original choice of £M3 in 1976 was influenced by the fact that in the early 1970s it appeared to give leading information about the behaviour of inflation. As Figure 1.2 shows, there is a close correlation between £M3 in 1972-73 and the subsequent surge in inflation in 1974-75. The rise in inflation was, of course, to a large extent due to the rise in oil prices and for this reason the correlation may be spurious. Maybe largely because of this correlation, studies examining the relation between monetary aggregates and inflation in the 1960s and 1970s generally came up with the conclusion that broader measures of money were better predictors of future inflation[7].

The experience of the 1980s provided contrary indications. As noted above, the narrow aggregates now appeared to give most information about subsequent inflation. But just as the £M3/inflation relationship in the early 1970s may have been largely spurious, this relationship between the narrow aggregates and inflation in the later period may also have been so. Examining the relationship between narrow money and inflation over a longer time period (Figure 4.2) shows little sign of a correlation in earlier periods. Indeed, narrow money growth appeared to be most closely correlated with inflation in the same time period. Furthermore, the surge in inflation in 1979, referred to by Lawson, was, to a large extent, the result of the switch from direct to indirect taxation (especially VAT) in the 1979 Budget and the second oil price shock. Mills and Stephenson[8] found that, after allowing for these two effects, MO's behaviour actually gave misleading information about future inflation. Nevertheless, the Treasury did feel confident in the role of MO.

Figure 4.1: M0 and inflation, 1976 to 1985

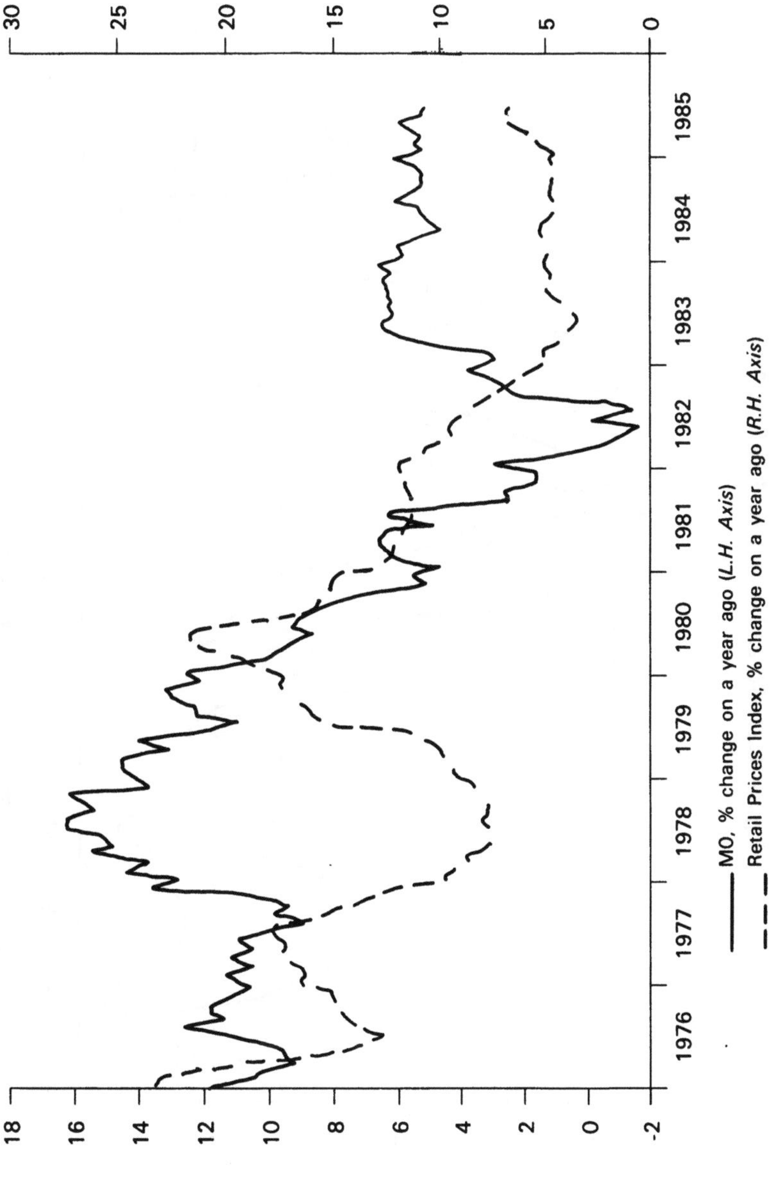

Figure 4.2: MO and inflation, 1961 to 1985

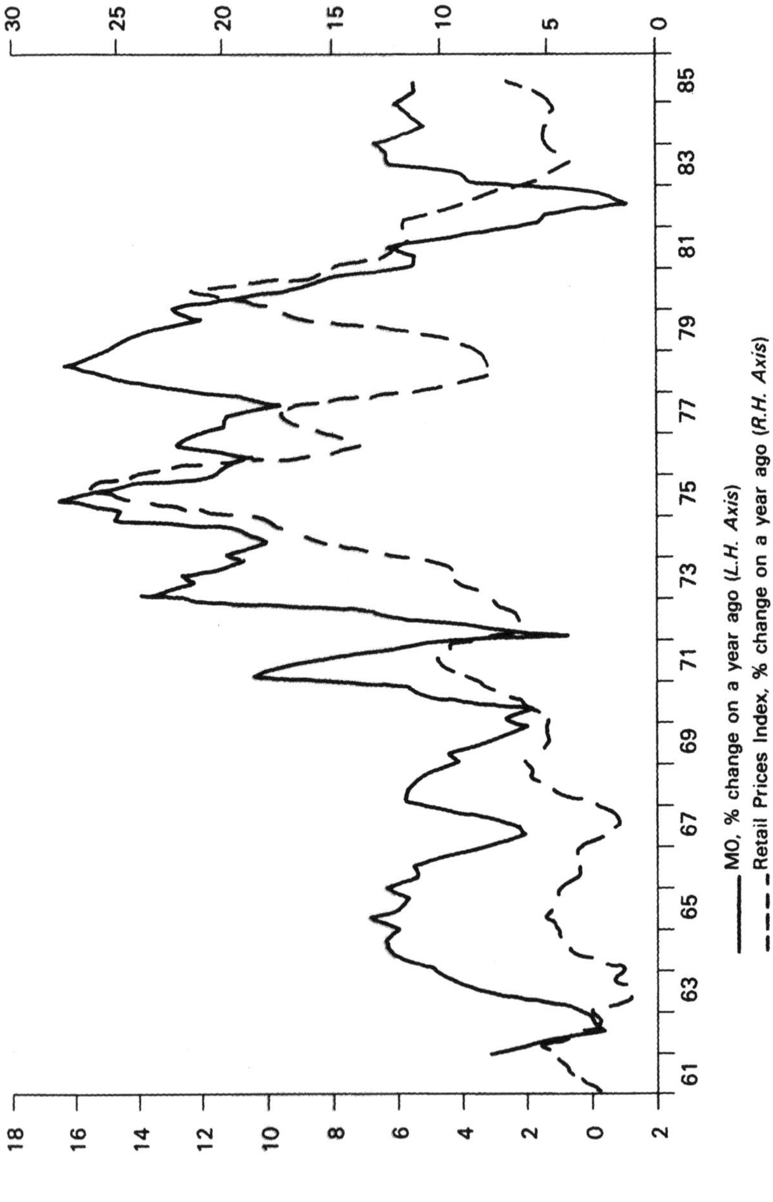

(iii) Explaining the behaviour of MO

If there was some doubt about MO's ability to predict future inflation, concern about the extent to which its behaviour could be explained was even more acute. Shortly before the Chancellor began to comment on the merits of MO, the Bank of England had published an article 'Recent Changes in the Use of Cash' which had concluded that 'structural changes imply that movements in cash are unlikely to be helpful as a guide to general economic or financial conditions'[9]. As cash comprises the largest part of MO (98½%, on average, in 1984/85), the inference that targetting MO would make little sense was easy to make. The Bank found that the demand for cash could not be easily explained by reference to other economic variables: indeed, its forecasts had consistently over-estimated the demand for cash for a number of years. Johnston's Treasury working paper[10], came to the different conclusion that a satisfactory explanation of MO's behaviour could be achieved by reference to a few key economic variables. Moreover, in contrast to the Bank of England's study, the Treasury found that MO was sensitive to interest rate movements. We summarise below the arguments concerning MO's behaviour.

Bank of England explanations of MO behaviour

The Bank work on changes in the use of cash started with the observation that there appeared to be a break in the trend of the ratio of consumers' expenditure to cash in 1978. Between 1963 and the end of 1978 the value of consumers' expenditure rose at an average annual rate of 11½% while cash increased by about 9½%. In the three years after that date, however, the average rates of growth were 11% and 5% respectively. A number of possible explanations were considered. First, that high nominal interest rates had led to economisation of cash balances. Second, that rising unemployment might have been important. 'Those becoming unemployed might have previously used cash to a greater extent than average and the lower level of unemployment benefits might thus have reduced the demand for cash'[11]. Third, the exchange rate might influence cash demand. 'In some small part this may be because of speculative demand, with exchange rate expectations playing a role. In addition, a large migrant population making transfer payments abroad and the increasing popularity of foreign travel may help to explain this effect'[12]. Fourth, was the increased use of banking services. In the late seventies and early eighties, the movement away from cash as a method of paying wages and salaries and as a medium for making consumer payments seemed to gain momentum.

These four factors influencing cash demand were considered in some detail in the Bank study. The factor which seemed to have the most important role to play in explaining the reduction in the demand for cash from 1978 onwards was the latter one — the increase in the use of banking services. Although this appeared to be the most important factor, data on the change in the use of banking services were severely limited; and in the Bank's econometric equations for the demand for cash, the variables which were used to try to measure this effect did not prove to have a significant explanatory power. In the Bank's equations the only additional variable of the four mentioned above which provided any significant amount of extra information about the behaviour of cash proved to be the unemployment rate. However, even allowing for this, cash holdings could not be forecast particularly accurately.

The Treasury's study of M0's behaviour

The Treasury paper by Johnston developed the Bank work, aiming to obtain rather more satisfactory measures of the changes in the use of banking services. In Johnston's equations for the demand for cash and M0, four variables were constructed in an attempt to measure the increasing spread of the 'banking habit':

(i) the number of current accounts relative to the total population;
(ii) the number of building society share accounts relative to the total population;
(iii) the total number of cash dispensers;
(iv) the total number of credit cards.

Johnston found that trends in the velocity of cash and M0 were in fact closely related to the trends in financial innovation as measured by these variables (in particular, the per capita number of current accounts and building society accounts). Moreover, econometric equations including these terms proved capable of providing reasonable forecasts (in contrast to the Bank's equations). Johnston's equations for M0 included interest rate terms and he found that 'the response of both notes and coin to changes in interest rates is modest, significant, and reasonably stable in equations fitted to recent time periods'. In the long run, a one percentage point rise in nominal interest rates would reduce the demand for notes and coin and M0 by around 2%. The new equation, based on Johnston's work, which was introduced into the Treasury's macroeconomic model of the UK economy[13] had the property that the demand for cash fell by around 0.25% in the same quarter as the three month interbank rate rose by one percentage point, with the effect rising to a 1% reduction in cash demand after one year and a

2% reduction in the long run. The maximum size of the long run effect detected in the Bank study had been just less than 1%, but they had found that in many periods the effect was close to zero and not statistically significant.

(iv) Controlling M0

The question of whether or not econometric methods are capable of providing a sufficiently accurate explanation of M0 becomes crucial when the question of controllability is considered. There are three possible methods of control, which are considered below.

Interest Rate Control

Cash is supplied passively on demand by the Bank of England to the banks and, similarly, by the banks to the general public. No attempt is made to control the *supply* of cash. Such a method of control would involve major changes in the way in which the Bank operates and would, to say the least, undermine confidence in the currency. Thus, control of cash depends on the ability to control the *demand* for cash and thus the explanations of cash demand, discussed in the previous section, take on particular importance. As we have seen, however, even between the Bank and the Treasury this question is a subject of some dispute. The problem is highlighted by considering the question of the appropriate response to a too rapid growth of cash. Suppose cash were growing at a rate 2% higher than desired. The Treasury's parameters would suggest that, other things being equal, a one percentage point rise in interest rates would bring cash growth back to the desired level in the long run: about half of the slowdown would occur in the first year after the rise in interest rates. The Bank's parameters would suggest, however, that the rise in interest rates would need to be around twice as large to produce the same degree of slowdown.

The dispute over the size of this parameter begs the important question of how this rise in interest rates influences the demand for cash. The most direct effect likely is switching from cash to other monetary assets. Intuitively, however, it seems unlikely that any marked economisation of cash balances occurs in response to a rise in interest rates. Indirectly, of course, higher interest rates, through their depressing influence on overall economic activity, would be expected to lead to a reduction in the demand for cash. The combination of these two effects should be picked up by the parameters in both the Bank's and the Treasury's equations (in econometric terminology, these equations are 'reduced forms'). If we are correct in thinking that the direct 'asset switching' effect of a rise in interest rates on M0 is unlikely to be particularly strong, the conclusion is that an interest rate rise produces a slowdown in monetary growth by depressing economic activity. This seems a rather curious approach to using a monetary target.

The Counterparts to M0

An alternative is not to control M0 directly, but rather to control the counterparts to this aggregate. The approach would be similar to that used for analysing £M3.

Expression of M0 in terms of its counterparts comes from the manipulation of the three following identities.

Definition of M0

M0 is the sum of notes and coin in circulation with the public, and held by banks (NAC) and bankers' operational balances held with the Bank (BB)

i.e. M0 = NAC + BB (1a)

Furthermore, the change (d) in M0 must equal the change in its two components:

i.e. dM0 = dNAC + dBB (1b)

CGBR Financing Identity

The CGBR can be financed by (i) an increase in notes and coin in circulation (dNAC); (ii) sales of central government debt to the banks, non-bank private sector or overseas net of Bank of England purchases of bills (CGD); (iii) by a rundown of the foreign currency reserves (RES) — selling foreign currency in the Exchange Equalisation Account (EEA) and using the proceeds to repay outstanding government debt will reduce the amount of government debt sales needed to finance a given CGBR; or (iv) other net sterling and foreign currency borrowing (CGOT)

i.e. CGBR = dNAC + CGD - dRES + CGOT (2a)

or dNAC = CGBR - CGD + dRES - CGOT (2b)

Bank of England Banking Department's Balance Sheet

The liabilities of the Banking Department must equal its assets: for simplicity, we shall say that liabilities consist of bankers' operational deposits (BB), cash ratio deposits (CRD) and all other liabilities (OL); total assets are referred to as BDA. So:

$$BB + CRD + OL = BDA \tag{3a}$$

and $$dBB + dCRD + dOL = dBDA \tag{3b}$$

or $$dBB = dBDA - dCRD - dOL \tag{3c}$$

Substituting expressions (2b) and (3c) into equation (1b) gives:

$$dMO = CGBR - CGD + dRES - CGOT + dBDA - dCRD - dOL$$

That is, the increase in MO is equal to the central government's borrowing requirement minus sales of central government debt to banks, non-banks and overseas (net of Bank purchases of bills), plus the change in foreign currency reserves (and the remaining counterparts which will, in practice, be less important).

Viewing MO in this way highlights the fact that the change in MO depends on the extent to which shortages in the money market — reflecting the CGBR minus sales of government debt and the change in the foreign currency reserves — are offset by Bank purchases of bills. (Chapter 6 explains in detail the significance of such flows for money market shortages). The framework might be useful with a system designed to control banks' operational deposits: the Swiss, for example, use a similar type of approach when analysing the monetary base. We discuss such systems of monetary base control in the next section.

Monetary Base Control

The amount of cash in circulation is determined entirely by the public's demand for it and it would be unrealistic for the authorities to try to influence the amount of cash in circulation by restricting supply. There is, however, the possibility of controlling the level of bankers' balances from the supply side.

Two types of bankers' balance (or deposits) are kept at the Bank. The first type, *cash ratio deposits*, are non-interest bearing deposits which all institutions in the monetary sector must keep with the Bank. They are essentially a tax on the members of the monetary sector and are designed to provide income and resources for the Bank. They do not form any part of a system of monetary control. The level is adjusted twice a year, normally on the third Monday after the April and October make-up days, and is at the rate of half of one percent of eligible liabilities (for details of the calculation of eligible liabilities, see the Glossary). This category of bankers' deposits is not included in the calculation of M0.

The second type of deposits, *operational deposits*, are deposits of the London Clearing Banks (LCBs) which are used for settling payments between themselves and the Bank of England. As is explained in more detail in Chapter 6, the Bank generally aims to offset flows in the money market on a daily basis. By providing assistance to the money market in times of shortage (normally by open market operations in bills but also by lending), or by absorbing surplus liquidity, the Bank aims to leave the LCBs' balances close to their target level. It could, however, by deliberately providing less assistance than necessary, produce a shortfall of bankers' deposits. This would provide a depressing influence on M0 growth. There are no signs that the authorities have attempted to control M0 in this way.

As mentioned above, the inclusion of bankers' operational balances at the Bank of England and banks' till money as well as notes and coin in circulation with the public in the target measure of narrow money gave rise to some speculation that this might be designed to ease the way to a system of monetary base control. Indeed, M0 has been termed the *wide monetary base* as it includes all three possible components of a measure of the monetary base. Narrower definitions would include just bankers' operational deposits at the Bank of England or these deposits plus banks' till money.

The concept of a monetary base scheme is that banks keep a certain proportion of their deposits as monetary base because there is a mandatory requirement on them to do so or because they can be relied on to do so over a period for prudential reasons. With a mandatory system the authorities could, by controlling the amount of monetary base in existence, control the total growth of the money supply (as this would be a specified multiple of the monetary base). With a non-mandatory system, the authorities could use the signal provided by variations in the amount of monetary base as a leading indicator of developments in broader measures of money and, hence, as a trigger for changing interest rates.

Non-mandatory schemes

Since 1981, banks have been free to hold whatever level of operational deposits they think suitable. The Chancellor pointed out in his March 1981

Budget speech that this system could permit a gradual evolution to monetary base control as the authorities would be able to monitor the relationship between operational deposits and the monetary aggregates. It has become apparent, however, that banks' demand to hold such deposits is very low indeed. The average level of operational deposits in 1984/85 was £150m, only 0.1% of £M3. Moreover, the relationship between the level of these deposits and changes in other monetary measures on a month-by-month basis has not been at all stable. This is not to say that the demand for operational balances is not stable. It may be that such demand can be explained by reference to other factors apart from the size of a particular monetary aggregate. For example, the level of operational deposits may be higher during the main tax paying season due to uncertainty surrounding the magnitude of payments to the Exchequer and hence the extent of the drain on operational deposits (such influences are discussed in detail in Chapter 6).

The lack of evidence of stability on the relationship between operational deposits and other monetary measures casts doubt on the efficacy of a non-mandatory monetary base system designed to provide signals for changes in interest rates. In any case, the behaviour of operational deposits, even if it were related in a known fashion to changes in other measures of money, might not give much of a leading indication of developments in the monetary aggregates. Although the level of operational deposits can be observed daily by the Bank, it has weekly returns from a sample of banks which can be used to give an indication of developments in other monetary measures. The improvement in the timeliness of information would, therefore, be marginal. Furthermore, it is questionable whether the authorities would wish to react week-by-week, let alone day-by-day, to changes in the monetary aggregates. Over such a short time scale, it is impossible to be certain about changes in deposits due purely to seasonal variations: the Bank would presumably react to seasonally adjusted developments.

Mandatory schemes

There also remain considerable doubts about the efficacy of a mandatory monetary base system. The essence of a mandatory scheme is that the authorities fix the amount of monetary base in existence. If the money supply grows at a faster rate than that consistent with the quantity of monetary base, there will be excess demand for monetary base. Although one individual bank can improve its base position by (say) selling bills and thus increasing its deposits at the Bank, the bank buying the bills from it will see a corresponding reduction in its deposits. If the banking system as a whole is aiming to be a net seller of bills, clearly sharp upward pressure on interest rates would result: only if the Bank buys bills (thus increasing the monetary base) will interest rate pressure be relieved. If the banking system as a whole aims to bring its balance sheet into line with the size determined by the fixed amount of monetary base supplied by the authorities, there are three possible adjustments which could take place. These have been identified as:[14]

a) a reduction in banks' assets and liabilities;
b) attraction of notes and coin from the public (which would clearly only be a method of relieving the pressure if the definition of monetary base was bankers' deposits at the Bank plus banks' till money. Even in this case, it would be difficult to accomplish);
c) a shift between different types of deposit if different base requirements were attached to these.

The 'scramble' for monetary base (described above) by raising interest rates may help to reduce the size of banks' balance sheets. Loan demand may be depressed (although, as we have seen, this appears largely insensitive to interest rate movements in the short run), but higher interest rates could have the perverse effect of attracting deposits to the banks. The payment of interest on cash lodged with the banks would presumably be the principal way in which adjustment (b) took place. Similarly, encouraging customers to shift deposits from (say) sight to time deposits (if, as in the USA, the latter had lower base requirements) would require higher interest rates on time deposits. All responses to a shortfall of monetary base thus seem likely to stimulate sharp upward pressure on interest rates. Similarly, in circumstances of excess supply of monetary base, interest rates could drop to very low levels indeed.

One response to such strict control is likely to be disintermediation of banking business (similar to the type which occurred in response to the 'corset'), with the banks developing mechanisms for channelling business off balance sheet in times of base pressure.

Actual experience with systems of monetary base control similar to that described above has, indeed, shown that greater interest rate volatility results. In October 1979, the USA moved to a type of base control, from a system which had been designed primarily to keep very short term interest rates within a certain range (i.e. a system similar to that currently operated by the UK authorities). Much greater volatility of interest rates resulted, even though the type of system allowed some reserve flexibility by allowing banks to borrow from the central bank.

The possibility of such greater volatility in interest rates remains the authorities' main objection to this form of monetary control.

Notes and References

1 'Monetary Control', Command 7858, (London: HMSO, 1980), p.iii.
2 N. Lawson, 'The Chancellor's Mansion House Speech', (H.M. Treasury, 20th October 1983).
3 N. Lawson, 'The Chancellor's Mansion House Speech', (H.M. Treasury, 18th October 1984).
4 See, for example, M. Friedman, 'The Quantity Theory of Money — A Restatement', in M. Friedman (ed.), *Studies in the Quantity Theory of Money* (University of Chicago Press, 1956)
5 R. B. Johnston, 'The demand for non-interest bearing money in the United Kingdom', *Treasury Working Paper Number 28*, (February 1984).
6 N. Lawson, 'The Chancellor's Mansion House Speech', (H.M. Treasury, 20th October 1983).
7 See, for example, T. C. Mills, 'The Information Content of Monetary Aggregates', *Bulletin of Economic Research*, (May 1983), pp25-46.
8 T. C. Mills and M. J. Stephenson, 'The information content of MO', *University of Leeds mimeo*.
9 'Recent Changes in the Use of Cash', *BEQB*, December 1982, pp519-529. The present author was part author of this article.
10 R. B. Johnston, op.cit.
11 *BEQB*, op cit, p521.
12 *BEQB*, op cit, p521.
13 H. M. Treasury, 'H. M. Treasury Macreconomic Model: Supplement to the 1982 Technical Manual', (June 1984).
14 C. A. E. Goodhart, M. D. K. W. Foot and A. C. Hotson, 'Monetary Base Control', *BEQB*, June 1979, pp149-159.

5 Setting Short Term Interest Rates: the Policy Process

In Chapter 2, when discussing the development of the MTFS, we stated that the authorities take into account 'all the available evidence' when assessing the relative 'tightness' or 'laxity' of monetary policy. Although the behaviour of the monetary aggregates remains of primary importance in the assessment of conditions, supplementary information is taken into account: in particular, this includes the behaviour of the exchange rate. Inflation (and inflationary expectations), asset prices and the state of the real economy are also considered. All these factors influence the authorities' judgement on the appropriate level of interest rates. The authorities operate, however, in an environment which is strongly influenced by market forces. The result is that 'the level of short term interest rates at any time is determined by the interaction between the markets and the authorities'[1]. (The ways in which the authorities can influence the level of interest rates are discussed in the next chapter). In this chapter we aim to outline in more detail the factors currently taken into account by the authorities when they decide on the appropriate level of interest rates. It is convenient to discuss these under three key headings: the influence of the monetary aggregates; the exchange rate; and other influences.

It should be noted, however, that there is no mechanical relationship between these variables and the level of interest rates. The weight attached to different indicators has changed over time. Furthermore, there have, on occasions, been clear differences of opinion, even between the Treasury and the Bank, on the assessment of the stance of policy and the conclusions to be drawn for interest rate decisions.

(i) The influence of the monetary aggregates

Behaviour of broad money

It might be expected that growth of broad money faster than that prescribed by the target range will lead to higher interest rates, and that growth slower than that prescribed by the range will lead to lower interest rates. The authorities, however, have generally not reacted to the behaviour of broad money in this mechanical manner. As discussed in Chapter 3, it has been the experience of the authorities that it is difficult to control £M3 in the short term by varying short term interest rates. An examination of the interest sensitivity of the counterparts to £M3 indicates why this is the case. First, bank lending to the private sector appears to be largely insensitive to changes in interest rates in the short run. Second, higher interest rates raise the interest payments on the national debt and hence raise the PSBR. Third, higher UK interest rates may lead to a switch into sterling from foreign currencies leading to expansionary 'external and foreign currency' counterparts. Fourth, if higher interest rates are seen merely as the precursor of yet higher rates to come, the government will find it difficult to fund its borrowing requirement. Sales of conventional gilt-edged stock, in particular, depend crucially on expectations of future interest rates (see Chapter 8).

Higher short term interest rates, if maintained, may help control £M3 in the long run. Suppose, for example, the authorities maintain a high level of short term interest rates and that it is viewed in the markets as being a feature of a successful medium term anti-inflation policy. In that environment, longer term interest rates (reflecting longer term inflationary expectations) might be expected to be lower than short term rates. The term structure of interest rates thus becomes 'downward sloping' (see Chapter 8). This could be expected to induce (corporate) borrowers to borrow for longer maturities (at lower interest rates) in the bond market. In this way, the pace of bank lending to the private sector may be moderated.

The evidence on the efficacy of such a technique is, however, limited. Indeed, it may well be that 'engineering' a downward sloping term structure in this way can produce perverse results. In particular, high short term interest rates may lead to a greater desire to hold short term deposits rather than, say, gilt-edged stock. Certainly, the authorities accept that the deposits included in the broader measures of money and liquidity have been attractive homes for savings balances in the recent past. In the words of the 1985/86 *FSBR*, the

> build-up of wider liquidity seems to have reflected an increase in the demand for liquid assets as a form of savings. It has been consistent with lower inflation and a steady decline in the growth of money GDP. As a result, the significance of the broad aggregates as monetary indicators has somewhat diminished.

Of course, this was only partly due to 'term structure' considerations. Also important in increasing the attractiveness of the deposits included in the wider measures of liquidity was the increased competition between the banks and the building societies in the area of personal savings: this led to the development of a much wider and more attractive range of savings media. Furthermore, the liberalisation of the financial system has enabled households to increase both their borrowing and their holding of liquid financial assets. One manifestation of this has been the increased extent of 'equity withdrawal' from the housing market.

Equity withdrawal is said to occur if net new loans for house purchase exceed net private sector expenditure on housing. Bank estimates[2] suggest that this amounted to more than £7bn in 1984. The excess lending could have been used for a variety of purposes — to repay other borrowing, to finance interest payments on existing borrowing, to increase holdings of other assets (financial or real), or to sustain consumption.

In the circumstances of the mid-1980s it thus appears that the usefulness of £M3, and the broad measures of money and liquidity more generally, in giving signals for changes in interest rates is highly questionable. In this environment, containment of £M3 has come to rely predominantly on funding policy (see Chapters 7 and 8). In the Treasury's eyes, the behaviour of narrow money, particularly M0, gives a more useful guide to the appropriate level of interest rates.

It should be noted at this juncture, however, that although the authorities believe that broad money may not be particularly useful in giving indications about interest rate policy, the markets continue, by and large, to view £M3 as important in this respect. Indeed, during 1984 and 1985 there were a number of occasions when there appeared to be a fundamental conflict between 'market' views of monetary growth — basically rapid £M3 growth pointing to the need for higher interest rates — and the Treasury view — putting more reliance on the behaviour of M0 — which was less convinced of the need for a rise in interest rates.

Behaviour of narrow money

With this evidence of the lack of interest rate sensitivity of broad money, the authorities have come to place more reliance on the behaviour of narrow money — in particular M0, the target aggregate — in signalling the appropriate level of interest rates. Indeed, when M0 was first floated as a target aggregate, Lawson[3] commented that:

there is some presumption that the narrower aggregates might have particular relevance for short term interest rates while the broader aggregates might be more relevant for decisions about fiscal and funding policy.

As discussed in Chapter 4, however, the extent to which MO responds to changes in the level of short term interest rates has been a matter of some dispute between the Bank of England and the Treasury. If, as suggested by the Bank studies, MO responds only weakly to changes in short term interest rates, it may be difficult to bring it back into its target range by changing interest rates. Since the adoption of MO as a target aggregate, however, it has behaved extremely well. In the 1984/85 target period, it grew within its 4-8% target range throughout the period (with the one exception of the month of April 1984, when it fell slightly below the range). It has thus neither shown signs of excessively fast growth (indicating the need for higher interest rates) or unduly slow growth (indicating the need for lower interest rates).

(ii) Exchange rate

The authorities have consistently stated throughout the period of the MTFS that they have no target level for the exchange rate. It has, however, always been one of the key factors taken into account in the assessment of monetary conditions. For example, the high and rising level of the exchange rate in 1980/81 was taken into account when the authorities judged that in that period monetary conditions were tight, despite a substantial overshoot of the £M3 target range. Mainly due to the strength of the exchange rate, minimum lending rate was cut to 16% in July 1980, to 14% in November, and to 12% in March 1981: throughout the period £M3 grew above its target range.

From early 1981 to early 1985, however, sterling's exchange rate was on a declining trend. This period saw four occasions of acute exchange rate weakness, each of which led to a sharp rise in short term interest rates. In the autumn 1981 exchange rate crisis, base rates rose in two stages from 12% to 16%; in the winter of 1982/83 from 9% to 11%; in July 1984 from 9¼% to 12%; and in January 1985 from 9½-¾% to 14%. This succession of crises has stimulated the comment that 'policy was determined more by the rate of change of the pound, in either direction, and action was taken to check too rapid an adjustment'[4].

The exchange rate does, of course, reflect a large variety of factors and the authorities have attempted to isolate variations in the exchange rate due to domestic conditions from variations due to other factors. For example, the present author, with Charles Goodhart, undertook a study[5] of the factors behind the sterling/dollar exchange rate's volatile behaviour in the period 1979-81, attempting to assess the extent to which the movement was due to changes in the domestic monetary environment, to changes in monetary conditions in the USA and to developments in the oil market. The conclusion of that study was that the oil factor was rather less important in explaining changes in the exchange rate than were monetary factors.

One of the clearest statements of the authorities' attempt to isolate the factors behind exchange rate movements was made by Nigel Lawson, Chancellor of the Exchequer, in October 1984[6]:

> we take the exchange rate into account when its behaviour suggests that the domestic monetary indicators are giving a false reading, which they are not.

At the time of his speech, M0 was growing at the centre of its target range, and £M3 towards the top of its range, but sterling had fallen by 10% against the US dollar and 5% on its exchange rate index over the previous two months. The authorities at the time considered this weakness due to two factors not under their control: the 'abnormal strength of the dollar'[7]; and the weakness of (dollar) oil prices. Robin Leigh-Pemberton, Governor of the Bank, commented later that[8]:

> neither of those two factors are directly within our control... I think it is perfectly reasonable in those circumstances to accept a fall in the exchange rate without tightening domestic policy to counter it.

Perhaps because of the authorities' attempt in the Autumn of 1984 to discount the importance of the exchange rate, and their willingness to see a quick reversal of the high interest rates of the Summer, another crisis followed in January 1985. Indeed, with the authorities' attitude to the exchange rate appearing unclear, the rise in interest rates in January 1985 was the largest seen in any of the exchange rate crises of the 1980s. The Budget in March 1985 attempted to clarify the attitude to the exchange rate. In his Budget speech[9], Lawson claimed that 'benign neglect [of the exchange rate] is not an option.' Moreover, it was stated that 'it will be necessary to judge the appropriate combination of monetary growth and the exchange rate needed to keep financial policy on track'[10].

Some light on what this might mean in practice was given by Robin Leigh-Pemberton when he was asked whether he would want to see monetary growth well within target before he would envisage a reduction in short term interest rates[11]:

> In circumstances of a weakening exchange rate, then I think it will be important to be convinced that monetary aggregates are working out preferably in the middle of the range or even lower.

The corollary is that monetary growth at the top of the range will be tolerated should the exchange rate be strengthening.

(iii) Other influences

Inflation and inflationary expectations

An important reason for attaching weight to the behaviour of the exchange rate is that variations in the rate can be expected to have a fairly direct impact on inflation and inflationary expectations. Exchange rate changes feed through with a short lag to changes in the price of imported goods, and with a longer lag to wholesale and retail price inflation. For example, the short term macro economic models of both the Bank of England and H.M. Treasury suggest that, after two years, a 10% depreciation of sterling's effective exchange rate will lead to a 2½% rise in RPI inflation[12].

Such a rise in inflation would, by tending to raise monetary growth, put upward pressure on interest rates as it came through. By reacting to the exchange rate movement itself, this rise in inflation can be 'short circuited'.

Real interest rates

Inflationary expectations are also important as they influence the level of real interest rates. The expected real interest rate is defined as the nominal interest rate minus the expected rate of inflation over the period. As mentioned in Chapter 1, however, at times of high and volatile inflation it may not be feasible to assess inflationary expectations with any degree of certainty. Indeed, this problem of assessing real interest rates was one of the reasons for shifting emphasis from the behaviour of nominal interest rates to the behaviour of the monetary aggregates in the 1970s. With inflation now lower and more stable, however, it may be that real interest rates can be assessed with more certainty. Indeed, the *BEQB*[13] publishes regularly various estimates of the real rate of interest, and estimated real rates certainly do appear recently to have played a more important role in official assessment of the stance of policy.

Various factors have to be taken into account in the assessment of real interest rates. First, the term of the interest rate. Generally, short term interest rates are focussed on, as it is very difficult to assess inflationary expectations with any degree of certainty over long time horizons. Assessing the expected real return to maturity on a twenty year gilt would, for example, involve the formation of expectations of inflation over such a time horizon.

Second, the question of the most relevant price index to use has to be assessed. Although the RPI is the most widely used, this can at times give a misleading impression of underlying inflation. Third, the tax status of the borrower or lender will be important. For example, an individual borrowing to finance the purchase of a house will be able to claim tax relief on interest payments, and thus the 'post-tax' real interest rate will be lower than the 'pre-tax' rate.

Asset markets

The behaviour in certain asset markets can also give an indication of the stance of monetary policy, although the precise impact which this currently has on policy decisions is unclear. For example, the behaviour of house prices may give an indication of the relative ease with which mortgage finance is available, and be an important influence on inflationary expectations. Indeed, the sharp rise in house prices in 1971 and 1972, presaged the more general rise in inflation in 1974 and 1975. Similarly, a sharply rising stockmarket may give an indication of easy monetary conditions. Again, experience of the early 1970s gives some support to the view that the behaviour of the stockmarket can give a leading indication of future inflation.

Real economy

As discussed in Chapter 2, the present government believes that the appropriate alignment of policies is for macro-economic policies to be used in the fight against inflation and micro-economic policies to be used to stimulate output and employment.

In the short term, however, it is recognised that a restrictive monetary policy can produce a change in the behaviour of the real economy. The way in which this has been presented is generally that, with monetary growth fixed, a higher level of inflation will leave less room for the growth of real output. In the labour market, high wage demands would price people out of work thus leading to lower employment.

A problem with presenting policy in this way has been the instability of the velocity of money, i.e. the relationship between monetary growth and nominal GDP growth. The 'trade-off' argument becomes much more difficult to present in this case. Sam Brittan, in particular, has advocated that, in such circumstances, it would be more appropriate to target nominal GDP explicitly[14]. Although the authorities have not gone so far as this, the 1985/86 *FSBR* presented the government's projections for nominal GDP growth and the relationship to monetary growth in a much clearer manner than previously. In the 1985 Budget speech, the Chancellor commented that the MTFS was 'as firm a guarantee against inadequate money demand as it is against excessive money demand'[15].

Notes and References

1. 'Monetary Control', Command 7858, (London: HMSO, 1980) p.6.
2. 'The housing finance market: recent growth in perspective', *BEQB*, March 1985, pp.80-91.
3. N. Lawson, 'The Chancellor's Mansion House Speech', (H.M. Treasury, 20 October 1983).
4. P. Riddell, *The Thatcher Government*, (Oxford: Martin Robertson, 1983) p.87.
5. C.A.E. Goodhart and P.V. Temperton, 'The UK Exchange Rate, 1979-81: a test of the overshooting hypothesis?', paper presented to the Oxford Money Study Group, 1982.
6. N. Lawson, 'The Chancellor's Mansion House Speech', (H.M. Treasury, 18 October 1984).
7. See the evidence of Robin Leigh-Pemberton to the House of Commons Select Committee on the 1985 Budget reported in Treasury and Civil Service Committee of the House of Commons, Session 1984/85, Eighth Report, *The 1985 Budget*, (London: HMSO, 1985) p.27.
8. Robin Leigh-Pemberton's evidence to the House of Commons, op.cit., p.27.
9. N. Lawson, 'Chancellor of the Exchequer's Budget Statement', (H.M. Treasury, 19 March 1985).
10. *FSBR*, 1985/86, para. 2.11.
11. Robin Leigh-Pemberton, op.cit., p.34.

12. See H.M. Treasury, 'H.M. Treasury Macroeconomic Model Technical Manual', (December 1982); H.M. Treasury, 'H.M. Treasury Macroeconomic Model: Supplement to the 1982 Technical Manual', (June 1984); 'Sterling and Inflation', *BEQB*, September 1981, pp.365-8.
13. See, for example, *BEQB*, March 1985, p.24.
14. See, for example, 'Chapter 6: The Case for Money GDP' in S. Brittan, *The Role and Limits of Government*, (London: Temple Smith, 1984).
15. N. Lawson, 'Chancellor of the Exchequer's Budget Statement', (H.M. Treasury, 19 March 1985).

6 Setting Short Term Interest Rates in the Money Market

The previous chapter discussed the factors which are taken into account by the monetary authorities when deciding on the appropriate level of short term interest rates. This chapter discusses the mechanics of the money market and explains how the authorities act to set interest rates. The distinction between interest rates set by administrative decision and those set in line with money market interest rates is made. A brief discussion of the change in the authorities' attitude to the relative merits of 'administered' and 'market related' interest rates is followed by a detailed discussion of present practices. The reasons for Bank intervention in the money market and its operational techniques are examined. The relationship between official money market actions and the determination of the clearing banks' interest rates is discussed in the final section.

(i) 'Administered' versus 'market related' interest rates

Up until the early 1970s, the Bank of England's Bank Rate was the pivotal interest rate in the money market. Bank Rate was the rate at which discount houses could borrow from the Bank in order to meet any shortage of liquidity. The Bank could, and did, make Bank Rate effective by open market operations. In particular, as the discount houses were obliged to take up the whole of the weekly offering of Treasury bills by the Bank, the Bank could, by deliberately overissuing Treasury bills, leave the discount houses short of cash balances and force them to borrow from the Bank. Bank Rate was the rate charged for such 'last resort' lending. Any rise in Bank Rate would induce the discount houses to raise their lending rates and this in turn would be reflected in the clearing banks' interest rates.

The importance of Bank Rate was recognised to the extent that this process became short circuited. From the 1930s, the clearing banks directly linked their interest rates to Bank Rate. The rate became the central rate in a system of 'administered' rates.

In September 1971 the new system of Competition and Credit Control was introduced. Under the new system, the role of quantitative controls on bank lending was reduced and greater reliance was placed on the role of market determined interest rates in the allocation of credit. The role of Bank Rate as the pivotal interest rate was reduced. In particular, the clearing banks ceased to tie their deposit and lending rates to it. However, Bank Rate remained as the 'last resort' rate for lending to the discount houses and, furthermore, continued to have a high political profile. In order to make the rate more flexible, but still leave it as a penalty rate, a new system of determining the Bank's lending rate to the market was introduced. From 13th October 1972, Bank Rate was replaced by Minimum Lending Rate (MLR). MLR was to be ½% above the average rate of discount for Treasury bills at the most recent tender, rounded to the nearest ¼% above. The rate was automatically determined by this formula and announced each Friday afternoon with the results of the Treasury bill tender. The right to suspend the formula was, however, reserved. If the Bank decided, with the approval of the Chancellor, to make a special change of this kind, the announcement would normally be made on Thursday at midday.

Although the formula-related MLR was considered a more satisfactory system at the outset, the new system itself was found to be lacking when interest rates became much more volatile in the mid-1970s: 'high and variable inflation was accompanied by sharp changes in interest rate expectations and in the term structure of short term rates'[1]. Lending to the discount houses at MLR was never for periods longer than seven days but that rate was tied to the three month Treasury bill rate. Such a firm link between interest rates for different terms proved inappropriate in such volatile conditions. Indeed, it was only a year after the formula was introduced that the first suspension took place (on 13th November 1973 when MLR was raised from 11¼% to 13%). On 7th October 1976 and on 3rd February 1977 the formula was again suspended. On the fourth occasion of suspension, 11th April 1978, when MLR was raised from 6½% to 7½%, it was stated that the formula would remain suspended until it was capable of being applied without change in that rate. After two further administered rises in rates, it was announced on 25th May 1978 that from then onwards MLR would be a purely administered rate.

Disenchantment with this regime soon set in. Changes in the official interest rate once again took on a high political profile and this led to problems with the conduct of monetary policy. Specifically, as soon as market interest rates started to move up, expectations of a rise in MLR were generated and the government's funding programme became difficult. Because official sanctioning of a rise in interest rates could be slow, a 'funding pause' could result: this led to problems with controlling £M3, which in turn could reinforce expectations of a rise in interest rates.

These problems, coupled with the Conservative government's free market philosophy led to a move back towards more market related official rates in the early 1980s. On 20th August 1981, it was stated that MLR would no longer be announced continuously: greater reliance was to be placed on market forces in the determination of interest rates, although the Bank would still aim to keep 'very short term' interest rates within an unpublished 'band'. The Bank said, however, that it 'might in some circumstances announce in advance the minimum rate for which, for a short period ahead, it would apply in any lending to the market'[2].

The next sections discuss in detail the present arrangements which the Bank uses in setting short term rates and assesses how the new arrangements have worked in practice.

(ii) The role of the Bank of England in the money market

There are certain key features of the UK financial system which must be made clear when discussing the way in which the Bank operates in the UK money markets. The most important is that the Bank maintains most of the accounts of central government and that these accounts are run with no spare cash balances. As the rest of the banking system maintains the accounts of all other sectors of the economy, any net payment to central government will produce a net flow of cash from the banks to the Bank. The banks will seek to restore their liquidity by drawing down their funds deposited at call with the discount houses. The clearing banks keep operational balances at the Bank which are used for settling the final position at the end of the day between the Bank and the banking system, and their drawing down of money from the discount houses will be designed to keep these balances at a 'target' level considered appropriate given the uncertainty of the daily cash flows to the Bank. The cash shortage in the money market is, in this way, passed to the discount houses. The Bank can offset this shortage either by buying bills or lending to the discount houses. Occasionally, direct assistance to the banks themselves may be given (see below).

Payments to government are not the only flows affecting the net position between the Bank and the rest of the banking system. The flows can be placed in the following six main categories.

Exchequer transactions

This category comprises: (i) payments to the exchequer net of expenditure by it; (ii) the proceeds of net official sales of gilts; and (iii) net receipts of sterling on the Exchange Equalisation Account (EEA). In all three cases net sterling payments to the government's accounts at the Bank reduces market liquidity. The Exchequer is broadly equivalent to central government. Thus if the government receives tax payments from, or if it sells government debt (gilts, national savings or Treasury bills) to, the public the proceeds will act to produce a reduction in the money market's cash position. Conversely, government spending will increase the deposits of the banks and reduce those of the government at the Bank of England. If the EEA intervenes to support sterling (i.e. it sells foreign currencies and buys sterling) then the receipt of sterling by the Bank will act to drain market liquidity.

The change in the note issue

If the demand for notes rises, the clearers meet the rise in demand by obtaining notes from the Bank, at the same time running down their operational balances with it. Thus a rise in the note circulation, leads to a money market shortage. Generally, the note circulation rises towards the end of the week (as people withdraw cash for the weekend and the banks anticipate the demand) and falls at the start of the week: thus on Mondays and Tuesdays the fluctuations in the note circulation generally raise money market liquidity and on Thursdays and Fridays generally reduce it.

Bills maturing in official hands and the take up of Treasury bills

If the Bank holds bills which then mature, repayment will come from the rest of the banking system so market liquidity falls. Similarly, as the discount houses take up Treasury bills from the tender on the Friday of the previous week, net payment will be made to the Bank from the rest of the banking system.

Unwinding of previous assistance

The Bank occasionally lends to the market or uses *purchase and resale agreements* (see section iv). The unwinding of such assistance (repayment of loans given by the Bank to the market/resale to the market of bills bought from it by the Bank) will drain market liquidity.

Clearers' balances above or below target

If the clearers' balances are above target — i.e. if the final clearing on the previous day left the clearers with balances at the Bank above those which they desire to keep in order to meet day to day requirements — then there will be a corresponding easing of the market's cash position.

Other flows

As well as acting as the government's banker, the Bank also acts as banker for other customers (e.g. overseas central banks and international organisations). Flows due to the transactions of these customers also influence the cash position of the money market.

(iii) The objective of money market operations

The objective of the Bank when operating in the money market is 'broadly to offset the cash flows between the Bank and the money markets'[3] and to leave the clearing banks within reach of their desired operational balances. In order to help this process the Bank forecasts the daily position of the money markets and makes its forecast available to market participants (via Reuters and Telerate). The Bank's initial forecast and the factors behind it are made available at 9.45 a.m. each day. Factors are normally grouped together under each of the first five headings given above (flows due to the behaviour of other Bank customers are never disclosed). Revisions to the overall shortage (although not the factors behind it) may be made during the course of the day. When deciding on the amount of intervention needed, however, the Bank also takes account of the reports of their positions from the discount houses and the major banks, and the behaviour of short term interest rates.

(iv) Techniques for relieving money market shortages

The three following principal techniques are used.

Outright purchases of bills

Under the arrangements first introduced in late 1980, greater emphasis is now placed on bill dealings as a method of relieving money market shortages (in order to create a deeper market in bills, the list of banks eligible to have their bills rediscounted at the Bank has been extended). If the Bank informs the market that it is prepared to buy bills, the discount houses will generally offer bills to it, specifying a discount rate, for each combination of instrument and band — or, if they wish, different rates for separate amounts within each combination. Bills are classified as falling into one of four (residual) maturity bands:

Band 1, 1-14 days;
Band 2, 15-33 days;
Band 3, 34-63 days;
Band 4, 64-91 days.

The Bank does not normally purchase bills with more than three months to maturity. The Bank decides which offers to accept: often the decision is the straightforward one of buying bills to relieve the estimated shortage. Purchases may fall short of the estimated shortage for three main reasons:

(i) because the discount rates are out of line with what the Bank considers the appropriate level of rates, the houses may then have the opportunity to submit revised offers. If the revised offers are still unacceptable, they may be forced to borrow from the Bank;
(ii) if Bank estimates of the shortage are unusually uncertain, it may decide to buy a relatively small amount of bills in the morning session leaving the final relief of the shortage until the afternoon;
(iii) because the discount houses believe the shortage to be smaller than that expected by the Bank and they offer a correspondingly lower amount of bills for sale.

The amount of bills bought in each band, the type of bill and the interest rate at which the deal was made are published after both the morning and afternoon sessions. Normally the Bank operates in the markets just before and just after lunch. Occasionally on days of very large shortages, it may offer to buy bills earlier in the day (10.00 a.m.) as well as at the normal times. The Bank may also provide late assistance at around 3.30 p.m.

Purchase and resale (repo) agreements

Purchase and resale agreements are occasionally used as an alternative to outright purchases. In this case, the Bank buys bills but agrees to sell them back to the market at an agreed price some time in the future. The technique is used for three main reasons:

(i) to smooth out a known future market position (e.g. arranging for the unwinding of the repo on a date of large central government spending);
(ii) to prevent a particular interest rate structure from becoming too entrenched;
(iii) it may be used when the market is reluctant to sell bills outright because of interest rate expectations. Thus if the market expects interest rates to fall, they will be unwilling to sell bills outright to the Bank. In particular, they will not wish to sell longer dated bills, the prices of which rise by a larger amount for a given change in interest rates. Another form of repo which has been used at times of particularly heavy tax receipts by the government is one undertaken directly with the banks. The repo is generally in gilts, although other instruments have also been acceptable.

Lending

Lending is only used occasionally under the new arrangements. As with earlier arrangements, however, the Bank can still, by refusing to relieve market shortages through bill operations, force the discount houses to borrow from it. This technique may be used when the Bank is keen to produce a change in interest rates faster than that which could be obtained by waiting for bill offers to respond to an initial rejection of bids by the Bank.

At other times the Bank may lend to relieve 'technical shortages' due to, say, over-subscription to a new government stock (for example, on 30th October 1981, the Bank lent £121m over the weekend through the discount window because of the heavy over-subscription for shares in Cable and Wireless). In such circumstances, lending will be at rates close to market rates and will be designed to avoid any distortion to bill rates.

(v) Techniques for absorbing a money market surplus

If there is a surplus, the Bank normally acts only in the afternoon to absorb it. Such operations are carried out in Treasury bills, of one or more specified (usually short) maturities. The clearing banks as well as the discount houses have the opportunity to offer Treasury bills on such occasions, as otherwise they would be at a substantial disadvantage compared with the discount houses in finding an outlet for surplus funds.

(vi) Recent experience with setting short term interest rates

Under the new arrangements the Bank has said it intends to keep 'very short term' interest rates within an unpublished band. Many people interpret this as a band for rates on Band 1 bills. The technique of enforcing the appropriate dealing rate is, as noted above, one of accepting only the offers for sale of bills which are considered to be at the appropriate interest rate or, if these are not forthcoming, forcing the discount houses to borrow from the Bank at a rate considered suitable by the authorities. On one occasion since the formal introduction of the new techniques on 20th August 1981, the Bank has announced a MLR. On Monday 14th January 1985, when the Bank wished to take a decisive lead in raising short term interest rates (in the face of substantial downward pressure on the exchange rate) MLR was announced in the morning. The shortage in the money markets on that day was expected to be quite small and thus the Bank would probably have had to wait until the end of the day to force the discount houses to borrow from the discount window and hence enforce higher short term rates. On that occasion, such a process was thought likely to be too slow.

1985 also saw a greater willingness to force the discount houses into borrowing from the discount window. The change of emphasis came shortly after the 1985 Budget, in which the Chancellor appeared to move in favour of a greater official influence on interest rates. On three occasions in the Spring of 1985, the Bank forced the discount houses to borrow from the discount window in order to prevent interest rates falling too quickly.

Although in 1981 the Bank said its aim would be to keep very short term interest rates within an unpublished band, and allow market forces a greater role in the determination of longer term rates, it has, in practice, been highly influential in determining the structure of rates out to three months maturity. In part this has reflected the sheer volume of the Bank's dealings in the market. As discussed in Chapter 3, the practice of overfunding the PSBR has led to persistent shortages in the money market which the Bank has relieved by buying bills from the discount houses. The result has been that the Bank has built up a sizeable portfolio of commercial bills (the 'bill mountain'). As these bills mature — or 'roll over' — rather quickly (they are of short maturity) this factor alone has come to be an important influence on the daily cash position of the money market. The overall shortage often amounts to more than £1bn per day in the main tax paying season.

One problem with shortages of this size is that the Bank's demand for bills can become so heavy as to depress bill rates relative to other money market rates and this can open up opportunities for round-tripping (see Chapter 3).

In order to reduce the size of the money market shortages, the government has encouraged the local authorities to borrow from the National Loans Fund (part of central government). This raises the size of the CGBR but leaves the PSBR unchanged. As it is only the central government's transactions which impact on money market liquidity, the higher CGBR tends to reduce the cash shortage in the market. (The other parts of the public sector bank with the banking sector. Flows between them and other sectors of the economy thus do not impact on bankers' balances at the Bank of England and hence money market liquidity).

There are other ways in which the size of the money market shortages could be moderated. As the shortages reflect, to a large extent, payments to central government's accounts at the Bank of England, an obvious solution would be for central government to bank with the private sector. For example, it would be possible for the tax payments made in the main tax paying season to be paid into a government account kept with the clearing banks (a similar system operates in the USA where tax payments are made into Treasury Tax and Loan Accounts kept with the banks). Another proposal is that the average maturity of the bill mountain could be lengthened (perhaps by the Bank switching commercial bills for longer dated bills with the private sector), thus lessening the impact of maturing assistance on daily money market shortages.

(vii) The interbank market

The discount market is the 'traditional' money market in London. In the last twenty years or so, however, large 'parallel' markets have developed. The most significant of these from the standpoint of the determination of short term interest rates is the interbank market. In this market, banks offer surplus deposits which they might have to other banks: banks who wish to acquire additional deposits in order to match their loan commitments bid for such deposits. These deposits are for a range of maturities from overnight to one year. Generally, the shorter maturities are the most actively traded. Rates in this market have taken on particular importance in the recent past for two main reasons. First, the UK clearing banks have come to rely more heavily on raising funds in the interbank market: their traditional retail base has been eroded, primarily due to the intensified competition with other financial institutions (especially the building societies). Second, many corporate customers now have loan facilities at rates linked to interbank rate. The London Interbank Offered Rate (LIBOR) has come to be widely used as a benchmark rate, deposit and loan rates being set on margins related to LIBOR. Many corporate customers now have access to both traditional base rate related loan facilities as well as LIBOR related facilities.

In the light of these two developments, the clearing banks have moved to a system whereby their base rates are now largely determined by the prevailing interbank rate. The three month interbank rate has become particularly important as the key reference rate which is watched by the clearers. Indeed, Barclays took the step in March 1984 of announcing that it would aim to keep its base rate within ¼—⅜% of the prevailing three month interbank rate. As Figure 6.1 shows, the relationship between the two rates in the recent past has been very close. As well as taking into account the current level of the three month interbank rate, the clearers will also assess the likelihood of changes in the near future and will examine the term structure of interest rates. Thus, for example, if interbank rates have fallen ahead of the release of a set of money supply figures which are expected to be well received, the clearers often wait until the release of the data before changing their base rates.

The term structure of interbank rates can give an important indication of future expected interest rates. If interbank rates are determined solely by expected future interest rates, then the current structure of rates can be 'unwound' in order to obtain expected future rates. For example, from the rates on three and six month deposits, we can infer the expected three month rate in three months' time; from the one year and six month rates, we can infer the expected six month rate in six months' time.

Suppose three, six and twelve month interbank rates are 10, 11 and 12% per annum respectively. Then, in order for the return from holding two consecutive three month deposits to equal that from holding a six month deposit, the following must be true:

$$(1 + 0.11/2) = (1 + 0.10/4)\,(1 + r_3^e/4)$$

where r_3^e is the expected three month rate three months hence. Thus, r_3^e = 11.7% per annum. Similarly, for six and twelve month deposits:

$$(1 + 0.12) = (1 + 0.11/2)(1 + r_6^e/2)$$

where r_6^e is the expected six month rate six months hence. Thus r_6^e = 12.3% per annum.

Figure 6.1: LCB base rates and three month interbank rate

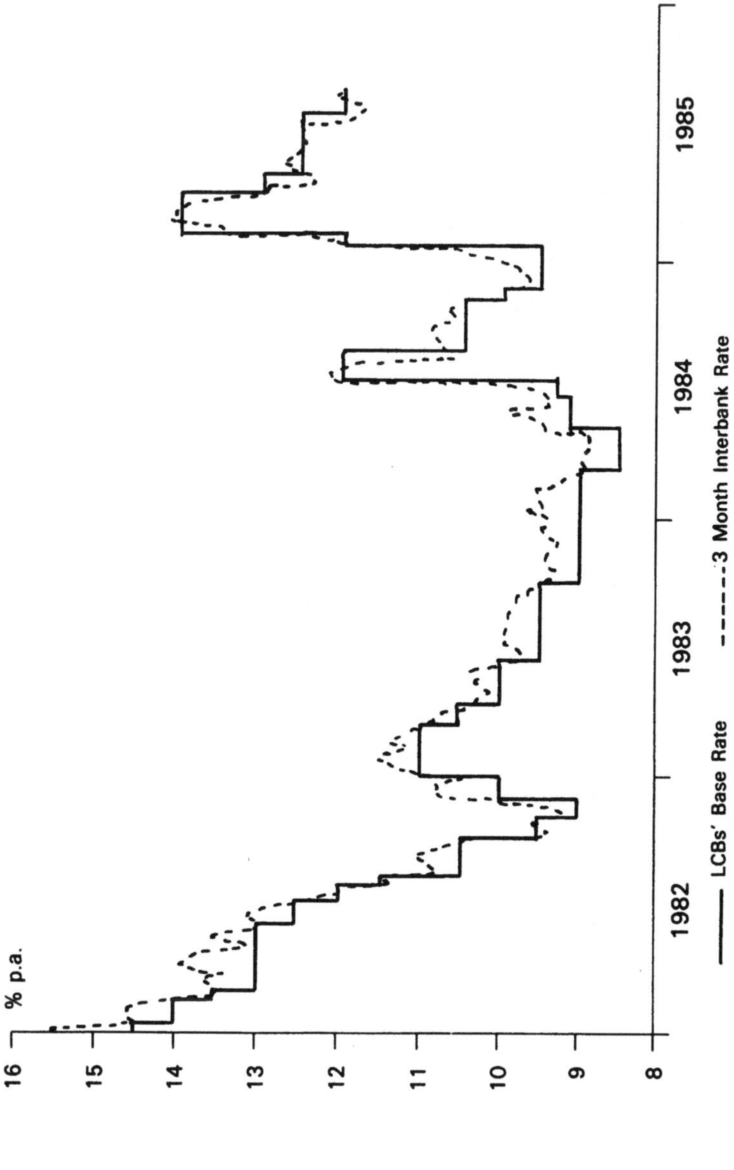

If the term structure of interest rates is upward sloping in this manner, clearly the banks will be less willing to reduce their base rates on the basis of the current three month rate. The futures market provides an alternative source of information on expected future movements in interest rates. The prices of the short term sterling deposit contract can be used to infer expected short term interest rates in a similar way.

Notes and References

1. A. L. Coleby, 'The Bank's operational procedures for meeting monetary objectives', *BEQB*, June 1983, p.213.
2. *BEQB*, September 1981, p.333.
3. A. L. Coleby, op.cit., p.214.

7 Funding the PSBR and Monetary Growth

As discussed in Chapter 6, the authorities maintain an important degree of control over short term interest rates. Their desire to do this rests on the belief that movements in interest rates have an important influence on the behaviour of the monetary aggregates, the exchange rate and the performance of the real economy. With the monetary aggregates at the centre of economic and financial policies, it is perhaps the first linkage which has been considered of prime importance in recent years. The link between interest rates and the behaviour of narrower monetary aggregates may, in some circumstances, be quite clear: a rise in the rate of interest on bank time deposits may, for example, lead to switching into these from non-interest bearing deposits, thus leading to slower growth of nib M1. Similarly, a rise in interest rates may induce switching into interest bearing deposits from cash, thus facilitating control of M0.

The link between interest rates and control of the broad monetary aggregates, in particular £M3, is not so straightforward. In the first place, a rise in interest rates may attract funds into interest bearing bank deposits and away from, say, gilt edged stock, thus raising £M3. In terms of the counterparts to £M3, a rise in interest rates is likely, in the short term (by raising the 'interest bill' faced by bank customers) to lead to an increase in the demand for credit. Furthermore, higher interest rates tend to raise the PSBR, also through higher interest charges. Thus, as discussed in detail in Chapter 3, short term control over £M3 by means of variations in interest rates may not be feasible.

Indeed, in terms of the counterparts to £M3 growth only sales of government debt to the non-bank private sector are controllable, to any extent, by the actions of the authorities on a month-to-month basis: short term control of the PSBR seems virtually impossible; the demand for bank credit is largely insensitive to the actions of the authorities on a month-to-month basis (even with a system of direct controls); and external counterparts and net non-deposit liabilities are very volatile month to month. The funding programme is capable of some short term management by the authorities. Their influence should not, however, be exaggerated. In the market for government debt, as in the money markets, the authorities act in an environment which is heavily influenced by market forces. At times, market expectations can be such that it is difficult for the government's funding programme to make any progress at all, let alone be subjected to careful fine tuning by the authorities.

During the 1980s, however, short term control of broad money growth took on increasing importance. Coleby[1], commenting on this, stated:

> From 1976 onwards [when published monetary targets were introduced]... it became increasingly necessary not only to attempt over target periods as a whole to compensate by debt management for variations in other elements of the monetary forecast, but to keep closely to target throughout the period so as to avoid disturbances to markets. For once the actual figure departed from the target path, the expectation formed that there would be a compensating change in the level of debt sales pressed on the market, with a resulting change in yields. Demand was either dampened, if the target was being overshot, or stimulated, if the target was being undershot, threatening an explosive departure from the target path, and corresponding volatility in yields and interest rates.

In short, there was a tendency for there to be periods of 'feast' and 'famine' in the market for government debt. The authorities made a serious attempt to overcome this problem, trying to set the course of funding on a more stable month-to-month path. This involved changes in both the types of government debt which were issued and in the techniques used for selling debt.

In this chapter we examine the range of instruments which is currently available to the authorities. Gilt edged securities (gilts) remain the most important funding instruments: Chapter 8 deals with that market in more detail.

(i) Types of government debt

Government debt can be classified as either 'marketable' or 'non-marketable' depending on whether it may or may not be sold to a third party. The total outstanding stock of government debt in market hands (i.e. excluding debt held by the Bank, government departments, the Northern Ireland government and the National Debt Commissioners) is commonly referred to as the National Debt: its size at the end of March 1984 amounted to £131bn. Table 7.1 shows the composition of the National Debt on that date.

Table 7.1: Composition of the National Debt

£ million, nominal value, end March 1984
Percentage of total in italic

Sterling Non Marketable Debt:		
National Savings: index linked	4043	*3.1*
other	16176	*12.3*
Certificates of Tax Deposit	2465	*1.9*
Other	3643	*2.7*
Sterling Marketable Debt:		
Treasury Bills	1426	*1.1*
Gilts[1]: index linked	7033	*5.4*
other	93561	*71.5*
Foreign Currency Debt	2555	*2.0*
National Debt	130902	*100.0*

[1] also includes a small amount of nationalised industries' stock guaranteed by the government.

Source: *BEQB*, December 1984.

The nominal values of marketable debt, rather than their market values are shown (the market value of gilts was higher than the nominal value reflecting the general fall in interest rates, and hence the rise in its price, since issue). Government stocks formed by far the largest proportion of the outstanding national debt (77%) at that date. Table 7.2 shows the composition of sales of central government debt analysed by instrument in each of the financial years 1978/80 to 1984/85. In the next sections we describe each of the government's funding instruments in detail.

Table 7.2: Purchases of central government debt by the non-bank private sector

	78/80	80/81	81/82	82/83	83/84	84/85
Non-marketable debt						
National Savings	968	2238	4224	3034	3283	3096
CTDs	-913	405	401	837	-248	802
Other	-187	-149	-178	-	-	-4
Marketable debt						
Treasury bills	7	74	102	192	26	-175
British Government Securities	8328	8871	7146	4609	9774	9202
N. Ireland Central Government Debt	5	14	26	36	32	-19
PSBR	*10018*	*12680*	*8629*	*8865*	*9731*	*10166*

Sources: *FS* Tables 2.6 and 3.4

(ii) National Savings

National Savings form by far the largest proportion of non-marketable debt outstanding and in recent years have made a significant contribution towards financing the PSBR. A National Savings initiative' was taken in September 1980, with various measures introduced to increase the importance of National Savings as a funding instrument. It was thought that by tapping the market for personal savings in this way, pressure on gilt edged funding and on long term interest rates could be relieved. A target of £2bn for sales of National Savings in the 1980/81 financial year was set. At a time when inflation was still high and not generally expected to fall sharply in the near future, the initiative relied heavily on the contribution from index-linked instruments: these gave a return linked to the general index of retail prices. A new issue of index-linked certificates was made available to everybody aged 60 or over (previously such certificates were restricted to those over national retirement age) and the maximum holding was raised. In addition, the limit on monthly payments into the index-linked save-as-you-earn (SAYE) scheme was raised from £20 to £50. The target for 1980/81 was comfortably achieved (see Table 7.3).

Table 7.3: National Savings targets and results achieved

£ millions	**80/81**	**81/82**	**82/83**	**83/84**	**84/85**	**85/86**
Sales target[1]	2,000	3,500[2]	3,000	3,000	3,000	3,000
Result[1]	2,239	4,224	3,036	3,285	3,096	n/a
Comprising:						
National Savings Certificates:						
conventional	619	1,510	1,314	1,605	1,998	n/a
index-linked	1,285	2,095	-127	-330	-280	n/a
SAYE:						
conventional	-30	-19	8	18	0	n/a
index-linked	130	104	-28	-13	-11	n/a
Yearly plan	-	-	-	-	27	n/a
Ordinary account	-81	-38	32	32	-9	n/a
Investment account	450	675	956	799	397	n/a
Premium bonds	56	45	80	87	87	n/a
Income bonds	-	-	891	1,073	830	n/a
Deposit bonds	-	-	-	110	138	n/a
British savings bonds	-190	-147	-90	-96	-79	n/a

Notes:

1 National Savings are purchased almost exclusively by the personal sector; the totals in the table refer to total purchases by all sectors which are, in some cases, marginally higher.

2 The target was raised from £3,000m (set in the 1981 Budget) to £3,500m in July 1981.

Source: *FS,* Table 3.9.

In subsequent Budgets a target for National Savings in the coming financial year was announced. As the table shows, these were exceeded in each of the financial years 1981/82 to 1984/85. A variety of new instruments was introduced in order to maintain the popularity of National Savings. For example, an income bond was introduced to meet the needs of investors wanting a regular income; and instruments offering taxable interest were re-introduced (these generally pay a higher nominal interest rate and are attractive to non-tax payers). The Appendix to this chapter gives details of the various instruments.

Although the terms on which National Savings are sold are now usually varied more quickly, they are not generally capable of being used as a tool of month-to-month management of the government's debt sales.

(iii) Certificates of Tax Deposit (CTDs)

CTDs were introduced in October 1975: they are available to taxpayers generally and earn market related interest rates. The interest rate depends on the time for which the CTD is held, and is higher for larger deposits (over £100,000). CTDs can be withdrawn for cash (at a penal interest rate) although they are normally used in the settlement of tax liabilities. They can be used in the settlement of all such liabilities (apart from PAYE). UK industrial and commercial companies hold by far the largest proportion of CTDs outstanding.

(iv) Treasury bills

Treasury bills are normally of three month maturity. They are sold at a discount, the rise in price bringing a return to the holder as no interest is paid. They are allotted by tender each Friday and issued on each working day by the Bank. The discount houses have a traditional undertaking to underwrite the whole of the Treasury bill tender: historically, this arrangement provided a residual form of finance for the government, meeting any financing requirement not matched by sales of other instruments. As explained in Chapter 6, when the Bank receives the proceeds of the Treasury bill tender, a shortage in the money market is created. Indeed, deliberate over-issue of Treasury bills used to be the primary way in which the Bank could enforce Bank Rate: the discount houses, in the face of the shortage so created, could be forced to borrow from the Bank's discount window at a (normally penal) rate set by the Bank.

Since the mid-1970s, with the greater emphasis placed on control of broad money, sales of longer term government debt (especially gilts) to the non-bank private sector have taken on greater importance, largely replacing the need for the government to finance its needs through the issue of Treasury bills. Indeed, the money market shortages created by greater reliance on sales of longer term debt were initially relieved by buying back Treasury bills in market hands. The continuation of this process through the late 1970s meant that the outstanding stock of Treasury bills was reduced substantially. The weekly offering of Treasury bills was thus reduced to £100m, the minimum size thought consistent with the maintenance of the market. Currently the outstanding stock amounts to around £1½bn.

(v) Gilt edged stocks ('Gilts')

Gilts remain the most important instrument used by the government in its funding programme. They accounted for 77% of the nominal value of the national debt at the end of March 1984 and for 68% of net sales of central government debt to the non-bank private sector in 1984/85. The market in gilts is well developed and ranks as the second most active government bond market in the world. Turnover in 1984 amounted to £270bn.

Conventional gilts

Within the total, conventional gilts remain the most important type of stock. They are defined by a name, a coupon and a redemption date. The name is of no particular significance — Treasury' and 'Exchequer' are the most common. The coupon represents the fixed annual amount of interest paid per £100 of nominal stock. The coupon is normally paid in two equal amounts at six monthly intervals. The redemption date gives the date on which the stock is to be redeemed. For many stocks a range of dates is given: for example, Treasury 11½% 2001/2004 may be redeemed between 19th March 2001 and 19th March 2004. The maturity of stocks varies from those due to be redeemed in the very near future to those six stocks for which no redemption date is given. Conventionally, the maturity classifications are:

up to 5 years to maturity — 'shorts';
5 to 15 years to maturity — 'mediums';
over 15 years to maturity — 'longs';
no fixed maturity date — 'undated'.

The longest dated conventional stock in existence is currently Exchequer 12% 2013/17.

As the funding of the PSBR through debt sales to the non-bank private sector took on increasing importance in the late 1970s and 1980s, new types of government securities were introduced and the method of selling gilts was modified. We discuss next the new types of instrument which fall into three categories:

(i) index linked;
(ii) variable rate;
(iii) convertible.

Index-linked gilts

Again, these are defined by the same three characteristics as conventional stocks: name, coupon and redemption date. The market for index-linked gilts is not as well developed as that for conventional gilts. The first index-linked stock was announced in the Budget of 10th March 1981: £1,000m of index-linked 2% 1996 stock. This issue was restricted to pension funds, although in the Budget of March 1982, the ending of all restrictions on the holding of stock was announced.

Given the uncertainty about the real yield at which the first index-linked stock would prove attractive to the market, it was sold by auction with no published minimum price. The stock was, however, fully subscribed at par, thus establishing a real yield of 2%. There are currently eleven index-linked stocks in existence, all bearing coupons of 2% or 2½%. Their maturity ranges from 1988 to 2020 (three years longer than the longest conventional gilt).

Both the coupon and the capital value of index-linked stocks are, as their name implies, linked to the RPI. The method of indexation involves an eight month time lag. A 'base date' for each stock is set as that month which is eight months before the issue of the stock. The RPI for this month forms the base index. Subsequent coupon payments are derived by multiplying the (unindexed) coupon payment by the ratio of the RPI eight months before the date of the coupon payment to the base RPI.

Similarly, the final redemption payment is calculated as the ratio of the RPI eight months before the redemption date to the base RPI multiplied by 100 (the nominal value of the stock).

Variable rate gilts

Variable rate gilts were also designed to be attractive in conditions of market uncertainty. Specifically, in times of uncertainty about the path of future interest rates, they provided a return which was linked directly to short term interest rates. Interest was paid half yearly at an annual rate ½% above the daily average of the rate of discount on 91 day Treasury bills over the previous six month period. Three variable rate stocks were issued (two in 1977 and one in 1979) with maturity dates in 1981, 1982 and 1983. There have been no further issues, although the possibility clearly cannot be ruled out.

Although the stocks provided investors with a degree of insurance against rising interest rates, their price did not prove particularly stable (thus offsetting this benefit to a considerable degree). In part, the price fluctuations were due to the fact that the stocks were not actively traded. The size of each of the three issues was relatively small (£400m each) and they tended to be held by the banks. The absence of any substantial interest in the stocks by the non-bank private sector in the UK meant that their contribution to the control of £M3 was limited.

Convertible gilts

A convertible gilt is generally a short dated conventional gilt with options to convert at later dates into a longer dated stock at predetermined prices. The investor in such a stock thus has the choice of holding the short dated stock to maturity or converting into a longer maturity stock on terms which are known in advance and may, at the time of the conversion, no longer be available in the market.

In periods of uncertainty about the future course of gilt yields, when investors may be inclined to shorten the maturity of their portfolios, such an option on a stock is likely to prove attractive. For the authorities, the use of such stocks may enable the momentum of the funding programme to be maintained in such uncertain conditions.

The first 'experimental' convertible stock, Treasury 9% Conversion 1990, was issued in 1973: each £100 nominal was convertible into £110 nominal of Treasury 9% 2000 on redemption in 1980. Market values on that date were, however, such that conversion was not profitable and only a small amount of stock was converted. Most convertible stocks now issued have several option dates. For example, when 10½% Treasury Convertible Stock 1992 was issued on 10th August 1984, the dates and terms on which it could be converted into 9¾% Conversion Loan 2003 were:

7/11/85, £100 nominal of 10½% Tsy '92 into £98 of 9¾% Cnvsn Loan;
7/05/86, £100 nominal of 10½% Tsy '92 into £96 of 9¾% Cnvsn Loan;
7/11/86, £100 nominal of 10½% Tsy '92 into £94 of 9¾% Cnvsn Loan;
7/05/87, £100 nominal of 10½% Tsy '92 into £92 of 9¾% Cnvsn Loan;
7/11/87, £100 nominal of 10½% Tsy '92 into £90 of 9¾% Cnvsn Loan.

Generally, the conversion option means that such stocks are priced at a premium in the market. The size of the premium depends on investors' expectations of future movements in the term structure of interest rates. An overall downward movement in the term structure, or a tilting downwards, will render the option more likely to be exercised, and the premium will increase (see Chapter 8). The terms of the conversion on the stock described above, as in general, tend to become poorer the more distant the conversion date.

One stock, Treasury 2½% 1999, more commonly referred to as the 'Maggie May' was an index-linked stock convertible into a conventional stock (Treasury 10¼% 1999). It was issued shortly before the 1983 general election, at a time of uncertainty about the likely course of inflation and interest rates. If 'Maggie' (Margaret Thatcher, the Prime Minister) won the general election, inflation and interest rates were generally expected to be lower than if one of the opposition parties gained a majority. This uncertainty made conventional gilts less attractive; by offering an indexed stock with the option of conversion into a conventional stock, investors were given the benefit of protection against inflation (attractive if 'Maggie' did not win) as well as the option of converting into a conventional stock should the fears on inflation and interest rates be unfounded. The authorities benefitted in that the stock enabled the momentum of the funding programme to be maintained in an uncertain environment.

Appendix: Types of National Savings

A brief description of the various types of instruments is given below, based on the Department for National Savings' booklet 'Investing in National Savings'.

Certificates

Conventional certificates can be purchased in certain minimum size units up to a specified maximum holding (£25 and £5,000 respectively for the thirtieth issue). A new issue is generally made when interest rates on the existing issue move out of line with general market interest rates. Conventional certificates offer a guaranteed nominal return if held for their full life (normally five years). Repayments of principal, and interest, are free of all UK income tax and capital gains tax. *Index-linked* certificates do not pay an interest rate as such, but their capital value is linked to the RPI. Again there is a minimum size in which units may be purchased and a maximum holding (£10 and £10,000 respectively for the second issue). Certain bonuses are payable according to the length of time the certificates are held. All repayments are, again, tax free.

Save As You Earn (SAYE)

Conventional SAYE schemes are now only available to individuals who are entitled to purchase shares under a share option scheme approved by the

Inland Revenue, although they were generally available between 1969 and 1975. The Yearly Plan (see below) is similar in nature. The *index-linked* SAYE scheme, introduced in 1975, was withdrawn on 31st May 1984: this scheme became unattractive as inflation remained low and was not generally expected to rise in the near future. The system of index-linking was broadly the same as for certificates, with the value of each monthly payment individually index-linked. Certain supplements were payable, depending on the period for which the contract was maintained.

Yearly Plan

This scheme is National Savings' most recent innovation, being introduced in July 1984. It was designed to replace the index-linked SAYE scheme. Under the Yearly Plan, regular savings of £20 to £100 a month are used to buy a Yearly Plan Savings Certificate at the end of the year. Savers earn the highest return if they keep their Yearly Plan Certificate for a full four years after completing the first year's payments. For holders for the full period, the interest rate is that guaranteed on the date the plan was taken out. Returns are tax free.

Ordinary Account

This pays a guaranteed rate of interest for a full calendar year at a time on deposits which may be withdrawn on demand. The interest rate is paid at two levels, depending on the size of the deposit. In 1985, for example, this was 3% for deposits under £500 and 6% for deposits maintained above that amount during the year. The first £70 of interest per annum is tax free.

Investment Account

One month's notice of withdrawal is required for deposits in this account. Interest is taxable, but no tax is deducted at source. Depositors can invest from £5 to £50,000.

Premium Bonds

No interest is paid directly, but a pool of interest is used to form a prize fund which is distributed by weekly and monthly prize draws. The prizes are tax free.

Income Bonds

Income bonds were introduced in August 1982. A lump sum is invested and pays interest (which is taxable) monthly. Originally the minimum holding was £5,000 but this was reduced to £2,000 on 3rd May 1983. The maximum holding was reduced from £200,000 to £50,000 with effect from 15th March 1984.

Deposit Bonds

Similar to Income Bonds, these are also designed for investors with a lump sum to invest. The minimum holding is much smaller than for Income Bonds (£250) and the interest is capitalised on each anniversary date of the bond (instead of being distributed monthly). Although interest is capitalised before the deduction of income tax, it is taxable. The bonds were introduced in October 1983.

British Savings Bonds

British Savings Bonds were withdrawn from sale in 1979. Interest was paid half yearly, and was taxable, but was not deducted at source.

Notes and References

1. A. L. Coleby, 'The Bank's operational procedures for meeting monetary objectives', *BEQB*, June 1983, P.211.

8 The Gilt Edged Market

The previous chapter described the types of debt instrument issued by the government. This chapter deals in detail with the most important group of instruments — gilt edged stocks (gilts). We start by discussing the present institutional structure of the gilt market; this is due to change in 1986 and an outline of the new system is given. We go on to describe the methods which are used to sell gilts, emphasising how these have changed recently in order to make the government's funding more flexible. Finally, we examine the factors behind the shape of the gilt yield curve, emphasising the importance of interest rate and inflationary expectations and the government's funding programme.

(i) The institutional structure of the gilt market

The institutional structure of the gilt market before and after 1986 is summarised in Figure 8.1. It is too early to be able to say exactly how the new system will work, but an outline is given based on the proposed structure at the time of writing.

The system before October 1986

The Bank of England has the important role of managing sales of gilts on behalf of the government. It manages new issues, and holds a substantial portfolio of stocks which is made available to the market if conditions are appropriate. One particular firm of stockbrokers, Mullens, is responsible for acting as the government broker (GB). All the Bank's transactions with the gilt market are carried out via the GB. The GB, in turn, deals with a small number of gilt jobbers who act as market makers in gilts. They are able to take positions in, and borrow, stocks but are not able to deal directly with the public. Stockbrokers are used by the general public when they wish to

Figure 8.1: Institutional Structure of the Gilt Market

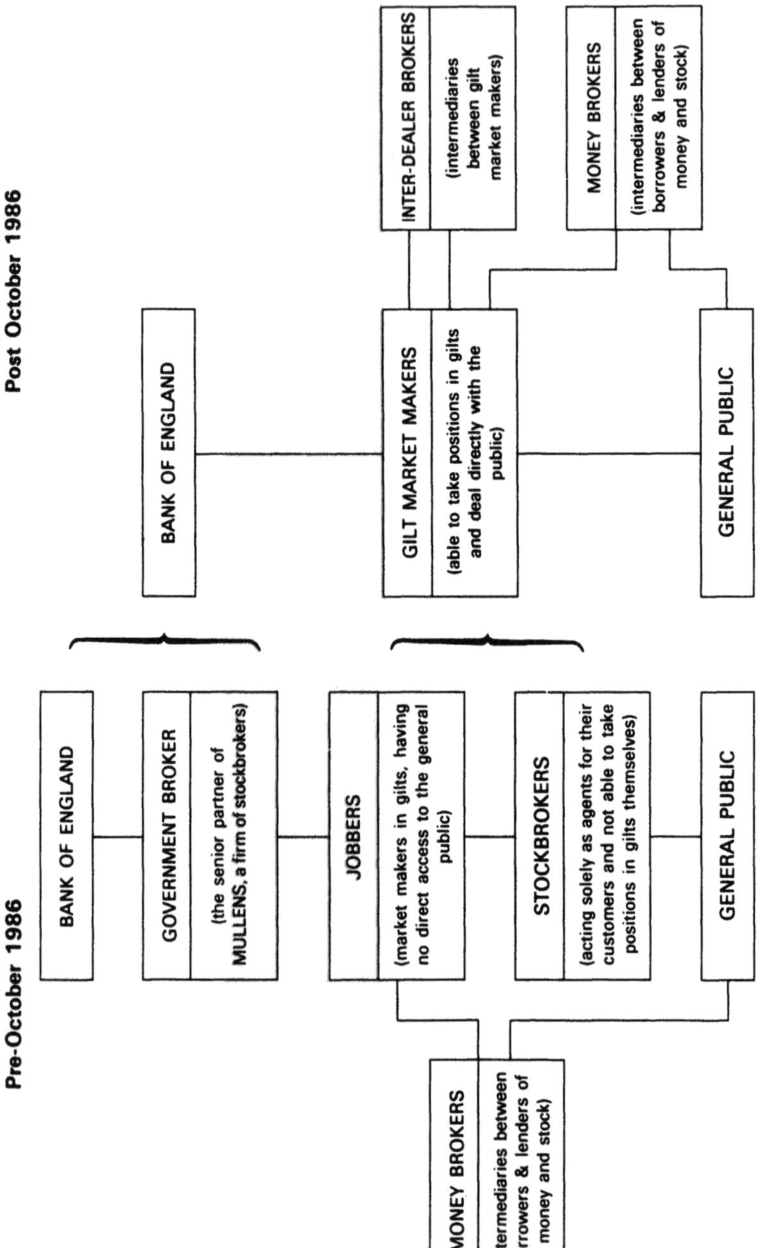

execute orders: the stockbrokers are restricted to act purely as agents for the general public, and cannot hold stock. This system is commonly referred to as 'single capacity' with jobbers only acting as market makers and brokers only acting as agents.

Brokers are remunerated on a scale of fixed minimum commissions, as set down by the Stock Exchange. Jobbers obtain their returns by the spread between their bid and offer prices and from any capital gain from their position in stocks.

The system after October 1986

After October 1986, the GB's role will be subsumed by the Bank, which will deal directly with the potential twenty-nine market makers in gilts. These market makers will be able both to take positions in, and borrow stocks (i.e. act in much the same way as jobbers in the old system) and to execute orders on behalf of clients (i.e. perform the function of brokers in the old system). The new group of market makers 'undertake to make, on demand and in any trading conditions, continuous and effective two-way prices at which they stand committed to deal'[1]. In return for this undertaking, the market makers are offered a number of special facilities, the most important of which are a direct dealing relationship with the Bank and the ability to borrow gilts. The market makers will be able to bid for any stock which the Bank has in its portfolio (particularly tap stocks, see below) and the Bank will buy stock from the market makers. Outright purchases by the Bank of conventional stocks are likely to continue to be predominantly for those stocks nearing maturity. For longer dated conventional stocks, the Bank will consider switches of stock with the market makers. In the index-linked market, the Bank is prepared to bid for stock of all maturities, creating more of a two-way market in this sector.

Two other types of institution will have a special role in the new system: Stock Exchange money brokers, which exist in the pre-1986 structure, will continue to provide facilities for borrowing and lending of money and gilts; inter-dealer brokers (IDBs), a new type of institution, will act as intermediaries between the market makers. IDBs will be an important channel through which market makers will be able to unwind positions that arise from their market making activities.

Figure 8.1 shows the broad structure of the markets both before and after October 1986. Figure 8.2 shows those institutions in each category — gilt edged market makers, stock exchange money brokers and inter dealer brokers — with which the Bank is, in principle, willing to deal.

A number of stock exchange brokers do not wish to make continuous

Figure 8.2: Institutions in the new structure of the gilt edged market

Gilt edged market makers

Aitken Campbell & Co. (Gilts)
Akroyd, Rowe & Pitman, Mullens & Co. Ltd.
Alexanders, Laing & Cruickshank Ltd.
Bank of America
Barclays de Zoete Wedd
Baring, Wilson & Watford
BT Gilts Ltd.
Cater Allen Holdings plc
Chase, Laurie & Simon
Citicorp Scrimgeour Vickers
County Holdings Group (National Westminster Bank plc)
CSFB (Gilts) Ltd.
Gerrard & National
Goldman Sachs Government Securities (U.K.) Ltd.
Hill Samuel Wood Mackenzie (Sterling Debt) Limited
Hoare Govett Sterling Bonds Ltd.
James Capel Gilts Ltd.
Kleinwort, Grieveson, Charlesworth Ltd.
Lloyds Bank Group
Merrill Lynch, Giles & Cresswell
Messel/Shearson Lehman
Morgan Grenfell Government Securities Ltd.
Morgan Guaranty Gilts Ltd.
Orion Royal Bank/Kitcat & Aitken
Phillips & Drew Moulsdale

Gilt edged market makers (continued)

Joint venture between Prudential-Bache and Clive
Salomon Brothers Sterling Trading Limited
Union Discount Securities Ltd.

Stock Exchange money brokers

Cazenove Money Brokers
Hoare Govett (Moneybroking) Ltd.
James Capel Money Broking Ltd.
King & Shaxson (Securities) Ltd.
Lazard Brothers & Co., Ltd.
LM (Money Brokers) Ltd.
P-B Securities Money Brokers Ltd.
Rowe & Pitman Money Broking
Sheppards Moneybrokers Ltd.

Inter-dealer brokers

Charles Fulton (IDB) Ltd.
Garban Gilts Limited
Mabon, Nugent International (Gilts)
Fundamental & Marshall Brokers Ltd.
Tullett and Tokyo (Gilts) Ltd.
Williams, Cooke, Lott and Kissack Limited

two-way prices in the new gilt market. They will continue to deal as agents for clients, but in the new market system will have the option of either taking positions in stock (although they will not be able to borrow stock) or dealing with their clients as a principal.

(ii) Methods of selling gilts

The offer for sale

The traditional method of selling gilts was the fixed price offer for sale. The Bank would announce on a Friday afternoon any new issue of stock, with applications to be made by the next Thursday. The issue price would be fixed at the time of announcement. Although this system worked satisfactorily for many years, it risked the possibility that if market prices moved substantially between the announcement and application dates, then the issue could be either not taken up at all or strongly oversubscribed. In February 1979, for example, gilt market prices moved up substantially between the announcement and application dates of Treasury 13¾% 2000/03. Considerable excess demand for the stock manifested itself in 'The Battle of Watling Street': the Bank's new issues department in Watling Street was swamped as potential investors aimed to ensure that their applications were made ahead of the 10.00 a.m. Thursday deadline.

Since then, the Bank has generally used a tender price method of issue. With this, stock is allotted to those offering the highest price, although the actual issue price is fixed as the lowest price accepted. The Bank normally sets a minimum tender price, although in some circumstances it may choose not to. For example, with the first issue of index-linked stock, investors were allowed to tender at whatever price they thought fit as 'there was no existing yardstick by which to judge the real yield at which such a stock would be subscribed'[2]. The normal outcome of the offer for sale is undersubscription. The remainder is taken up by the Issue Department of the Bank and is operated as a 'tap stock'.

The tap system

Tap stocks come into existence in one of three ways. First, by the Bank taking up the residue from an offer for sale (as above). Second, by the government creating small additional tranches of existing stock and selling these directly to the Bank. Third, by the government selling other stocks in its portfolio — the so-called 'unofficial taps'.

The technique of issuing further tranches of existing stock (known as 'tranchettes') direct to the Bank was first used in December 1980. With this system the Bank can be supplied with additional amounts of stock, which it can then sell as a normal tap. The price is set as the middle closing price of the existing stock on the day of announcement. Normally, the stock is available for sale on the next business day. Most often, tranchettes are announced on a Friday with dealings commencing on the following Monday. Tranchettes are normally around £100m to £250m in size and several issues are often announced at the same time. This technique enables the government to maintain the momentum of its funding programme when a larger new issue of stock might not be easily assimilated by the market.

Unofficial taps also come into existence in three main ways. First, the authorities might at times choose to buy stock, in order to stabilise a falling market. The stock they acquire in this way is then available for resale to the market. Second, they may facilitate switching into a new tap stock by being prepared to buy other stock in exchange for the tap: normally this would be with the intention of lengthening the average maturity of stock in existence. Third, they may obtain stock from the National Debt Commissioners[3].

Generally, the pricing of tap stocks follows two main principles. First, sales of tap stock acquired after an offer for sale has not been fully subscribed are generally at a higher price than that which was available in the offer for sale. Indeed, the Bank will generally aim to increase gradually the price at which the stock is sold, such that investors buying the stock on application will not be disadvantaged. Second, if market prices should fall generally then the Bank will not cut the tap price immediately. Rather, it will wait until the market has consolidated at a new lower level before cutting the price. Cutting the price gradually would risk the possibility of extrapolative expectations gaining hold, thus leading to potentially unstable market conditions. Having said this, the last two years have seen a gradual movement towards greater willingness to cut the tap price by smaller amounts, and more quickly.

Partly paid stocks

Stocks offered for sale can be either on a fully or partly paid basis, depending on whether all or part of the subscription money is to be paid on application. Partly paid stocks have become much more popular recently. Generally, payments are timed to coincide with periods when the government's need for finance is expected to be at its greatest. They are particularly useful in a strong market, when the government has already met a large proportion of its current borrowing needs.

Auction system

In the new structure of the gilt market, the gilt edged market makers will, in total, have a much larger amount of capital than the jobbers in the old structure. The primary market will thus be more capable of absorbing new issues by the Bank. The Bank has said that, in these circumstances, it will wish to examine whether 'some part at least of the funding programme might be put on a more regular footing'[4]. Many interpret this as the possibility of moving to an auction system. Such a system is used in the USA and involves the authorities announcing a quantity of stock which they wish to sell by auction, the price being set by the market. In the extreme, it is the opposite of the present UK system which may be characterised as one in which the central bank fixes the price of stock and sells whatever quantity is demanded at that price.

(iii) Explaining the shape of the yield curve

The influence of short term interest rates

There are important linkages between short term interest rates and gilt yields. One reason for such a link is that bank deposits and money market instruments are substitutes for investing in gilts. For short maturities (generally up to twelve months) there is a wide variety of instruments which give a certain nominal return. Investors will not be willing to invest in a gilt which matures in one year if the return on it is less than that which could be earned on a one year money market deposit. Arbitrage between the two markets will bring returns into broad equality.

For longer maturities, money market returns are not certain. However, market participants will form expectations of future money market returns. They will be unwilling to invest in the gilt market if the expected return from investing in a series of short dated money market instruments falls short of that return on a gilt which has a similar maturity. To take a simple example, if one year money market interest rates are currently 10% and are expected to fall by ½% per year over the next four years, then the expected total return from investing in the money market at the start of year 6 will be 54.56%, equivalent to an average annual return of 9.1% (see Table 8.1). Market participants will be unwilling to commit funds to the gilt market if the

Table 8.1: Money market returns

Year:	One year interest rate at start of year (% p.a.):	Capital value at start of year:	Average Return over period (% p.a.):
1	10	100.00	-
2	9½	110.00	10.0
3	9	120.45	9.7
4	8½	131.29	9.5
5	8	142.45	9.2
6	8	154.56	9.1
7	8	166.92	8.9
8	8	180.28	8.8
9	8	194.70	8.7
10	8	210.28	8.6
:	8	:	:
15	8	308.97	8.4
:	8	:	:
20	8	453.97	8.3
:	8	:	:
25	8	667.03	8.2

expected return from investing there falls short of those returns which are expected in the money market. Thus, an investor would not be willing to buy a gilt maturing at the start of year 6 if the total return were expected to be less than 9.1% per annum on average.

The example can be extended: if one year interest rates are expected to remain at 8% per annum from the start of year five onwards, then the 'break even' return between the money and gilt markets will fall steadily (see Table 8.1). At the start of the twenty-fifth year, the average annual return from investing in the money market will have been 8.2% if short term interest rates follow such a profile. Again, market participants will be unwilling to purchase a gilt which matures in twenty-four years' time if the average yield from doing so falls below 8.2% per annum.

Assessing the yield on a gilt over such periods is, however, not straightforward. All gilts have a coupon, which is normally paid semi-annually. In order to assess the total return from investing in the gilt market, an assessment of the basis on which these coupons can be reinvested in the future must be made at the outset.

The rate at which it is expected that future coupon payments can be invested is commonly referred to as the 'roll up' rate. One simple assumption would be that future coupon payments are not reinvested in the gilt market but are invested in the money market, at rates which are set out in Table 8.1. For long investment horizons and/or for gilts with high coupons this approach is unsatisfactory as the 'alternative' investment to the money market will contain a large 'money market' element.

The widely used measure of *gross redemption yield* also fails to deal adequately with this problem of reinvestment of coupons. The gross redemption yield (R) is defined as that rate of interest at which the total discounted values of future payments of income and capital equate to the current total price. Thus given the current price (P), the coupon payment (c) which is paid semi-annually and a gilt of maturity n (where n is the number of half years), then the following formula applies:

$$P = \frac{c}{2}v + \frac{c}{2}v^2 + \frac{c}{2}v^3 + \ldots + \frac{c}{2}v^n + 100v^n \qquad (8.1)$$

where $v = 1/(1+R/200)$.

This can be solved easily to give the value of R. It is, however, highly unlikely that all future coupons could be reinvested at this rate. Despite this drawback, gross redemption yields are widely used, particularly in the formation of yield curves (these show the relationship between gross redemption yields on stocks of different maturities). The gross redemption yield tends, however, to rise as the coupon rises: thus it is common to use only stocks with coupons in certain ranges when constructing a yield curve. For example, three yield curves are shown in Figure 8.3, which are formed using stocks with 'low', 'medium' and 'high' coupons respectively.

Another version of the yield curve is the par yield curve. This deals with the problem of different coupons by solving the equation (8.1 above) along the length of the maturity range to find the values of c (the coupon) to make P (the price) equal to 100. If the price is equal to 100 (i.e. the stock stands at 'par') then coupon and yield are obviously equal.

Many shapes of yield curve are possible. Figure 8.4 shows some examples, and the terminology used to describe them. Returning to our earlier example on the relationship between expected future short term interest rates and gilt yields, one would expect an upward sloping yield curve if short term interest rates are expected to rise in the future and a downward sloping yield curve if short rates are expected to fall. A rise in interest rates in the near term followed by a decline thereafter could give rise to the 'humped' shape. The yield curve would 'steepen' if short term interest rates rose, but expected short term interest rates in the future did not rise by a

Figure 8.3: Low, medium and high coupon yield curves

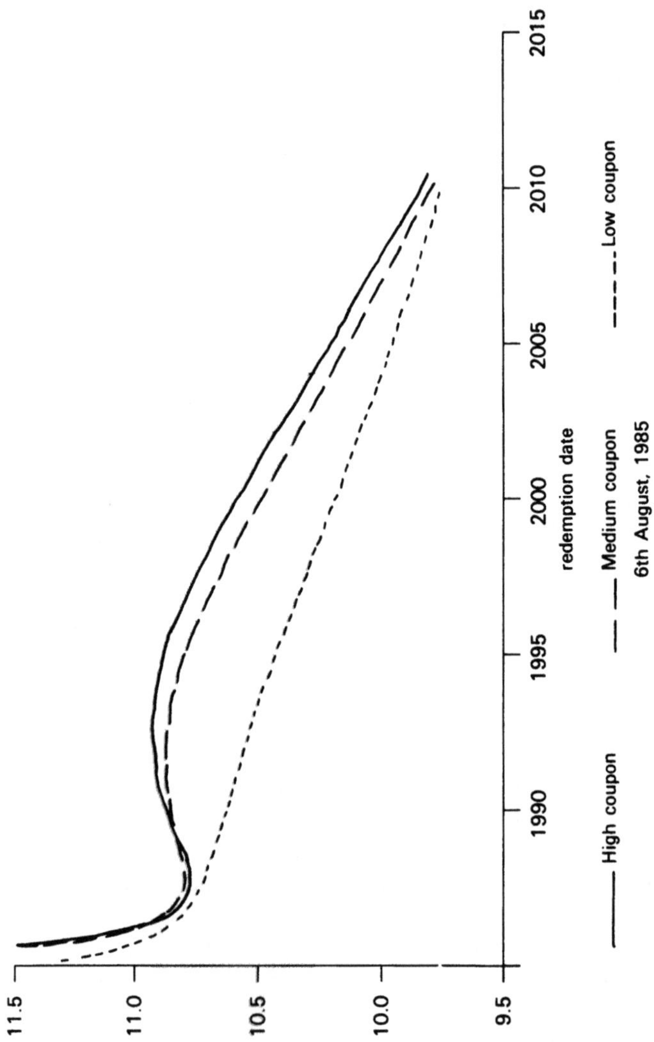

Figure 8.4: Yield Curves

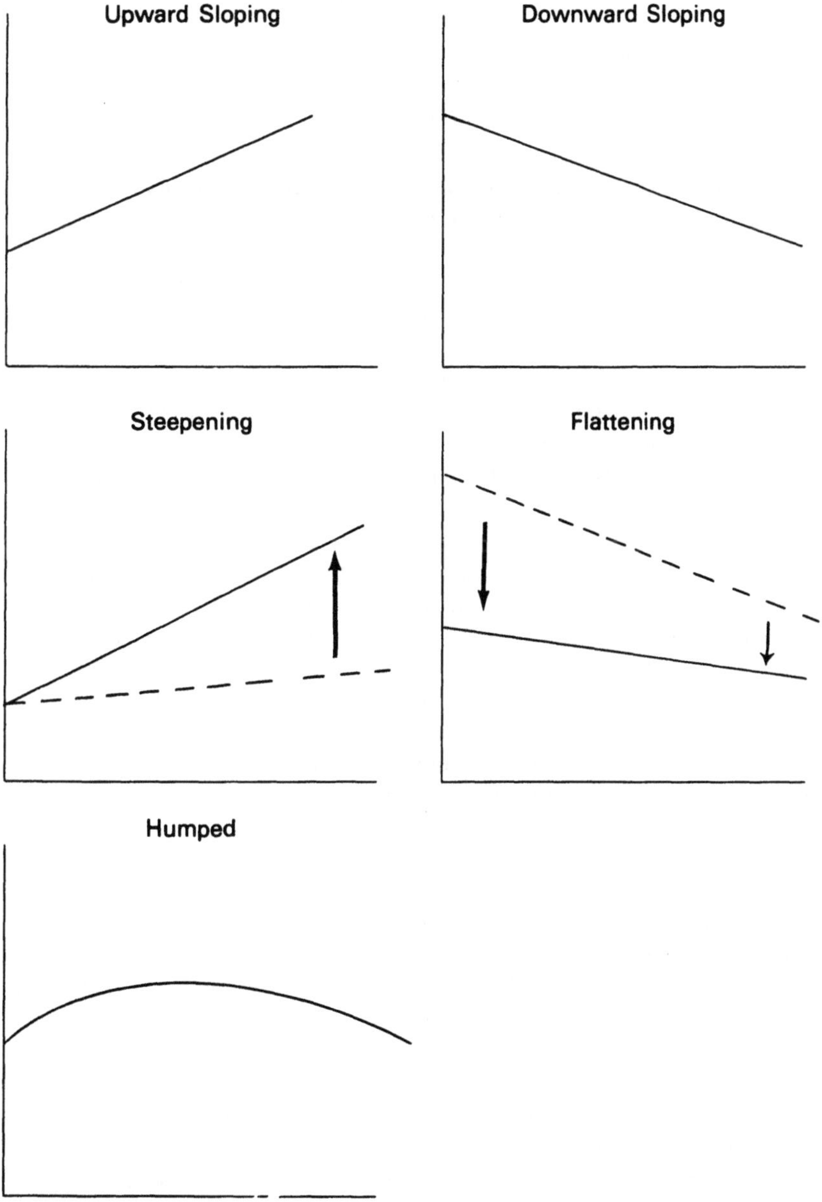

In all cases yield is measured on the vertical axis and term to maturity on the horizontal axis.

corresponding amount. Conversely, if short term rates in the future did not fall by as much, the yield curve would flatten.

Slope of the yield curve and the stance of monetary policy

On the basis of the expectational theory of the term structure of interest rates, it has been suggested that a downward sloping yield curve indicates that monetary policy is 'tight' and an upward sloping yield curve that policy is 'loose'. The reasoning behind this is quite straightforward. Suppose the authorities keep short term interest rates high in order to reduce monetary growth and, hence, inflation in the future. If future inflation is expected to be lower than current inflation, short term interest rates might also be expected to be lower in the future. On the basis of such expectations, the yield curve would be downward sloping. Conversely, if short term interest rates are low, monetary growth is expected to rise and inflation is expected to rise in the future, the yield curve will be upward sloping.

A simple way of expressing the slope of the yield curve is to take the ratio of a representative short term interest rate to a long term gilt yield. Movements in the ratio might then be used to interpret changes in the stance of policy[5]. Thus, in Figure 8.5, the rise in the ratio of long to short term rates in 1977 signifies an easing of policy, followed in 1978 and 1979 by a marked tightening. More recently, the fall in the ratio in mid-1984 and again in early 1985 signalled a tightening of policy. Although the slope of the yield curve may give some indication of the stance of monetary policy, there are other important influences on the relationship between short and long term interest rates. These can be conveniently discussed under three headings: volatility; hedging behaviour; and funding policy.

Volatility

Many holders of gilts do not hold to maturity. Certainly very few market participants assess rationally their expectations of future movements in short term interest rates and base their decisions about investing in the gilt market on expected relative total returns in the gilt and money markets over some long time horizon. Relative return calculations are performed, but these are generally over much shorter time horizons. The average holding period for a long dated conventional gilt is around one year. When assessing total returns over a holding period which is shorter than that of the maturity of the stock, variations in the price of the gilt become important. For a given change in yield, a longer dated gilt will change in price by more than a shorter dated gilt. The percentage change in the price of a gilt

Figure 8.5: Long/short interest rate ratio, 1976 to 1985

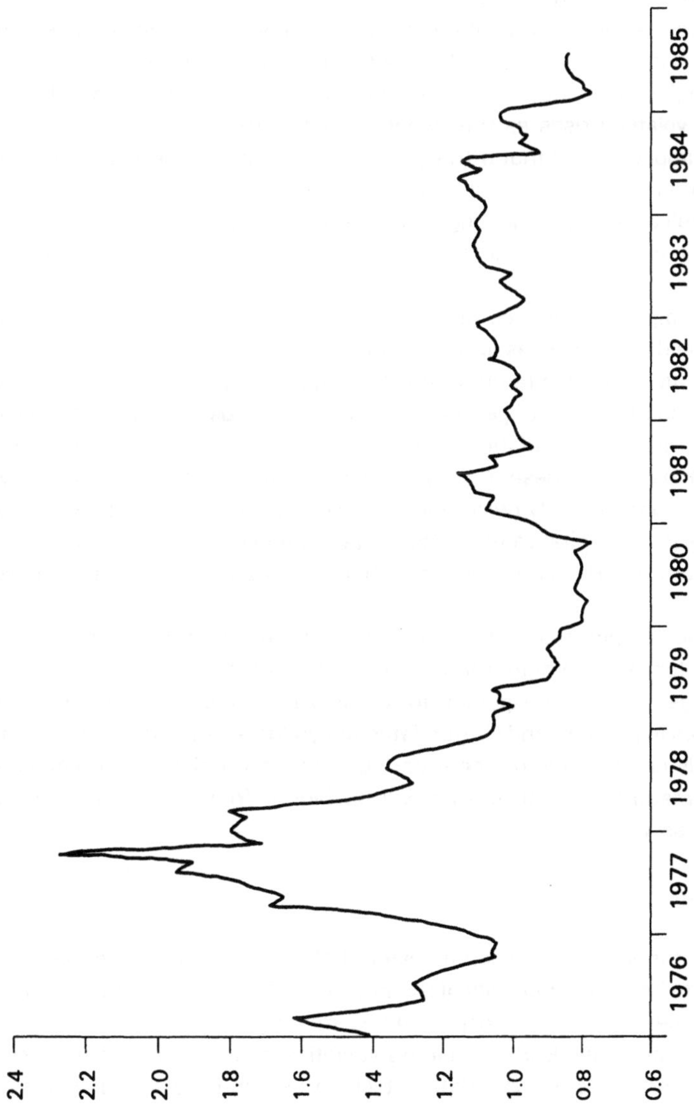

Ratio of the yield on high coupon long dated gilts to the three month interbank rate.

relative to the change in yield is referred to as its *volatility*. Consider, for example, a gilt currently close to its par value. Yield rises by 1% and its price falls by £5; its volatility is 5. Figure 8.6 demonstrates the way in which volatility was related to term to maturity and coupon in August 1985.

As well as the maturity of the stock, volatility also depends on two other factors. First, coupon: normally low coupon stocks have higher volatilities than high coupon stocks for a given maturity. Second, the general level of yields: volatility rises as the general level of yield falls.

The implication is that if the yield curve shifts downwards by the same amount in yield at each maturity, the higher volatility of longerstead, short yields fell by, say, 1% and long dated yields by ½%, then the smaller change in yield would offset the higher volatility and total returns would be equalised.

The empirical evidence on the relationship between changes in short term yields suggests, as would be expected, that yields do not change by similar amounts at different maturities. Goodhart and Gowland[6], for example, found that the change in twenty year gilt yields during the course of a month was around half the change in five year yields: subsequent work has tended to confirm these findings. Given that the volatility of a twenty year stock is approximately twice that of a five year stock, this implies a similar change in the capital value of the longer dated stock, and that total returns from both sectors in response to a change in interest rates may be broadly similar.

These estimates do not support the general view that investors should switch longer for a higher total return if short term interest rates, and gilt yields generally, are expected to fall. However, the relationship between changes in medium and longer dated gilt yields appears to be much closer, virtually one-for-one in recent periods. With the difference in volatility at these maturities, total returns will be higher from holding longer dated stocks as yields fall.

Hedging

The maturity of stock which investors hold will also be determined by any desire to hedge the maturity of their portfolio. Thus, life assurance companies and pension funds whose liabilities are long term generally wish to hold longer dated gilts. Banks, building societies and discount houses, on the other hand, prefer shorter dated stock. In extreme cases, these pressures can be so intense that the market is 'segmented'. Changes in the supply

Figure 8.6: Volatility against term

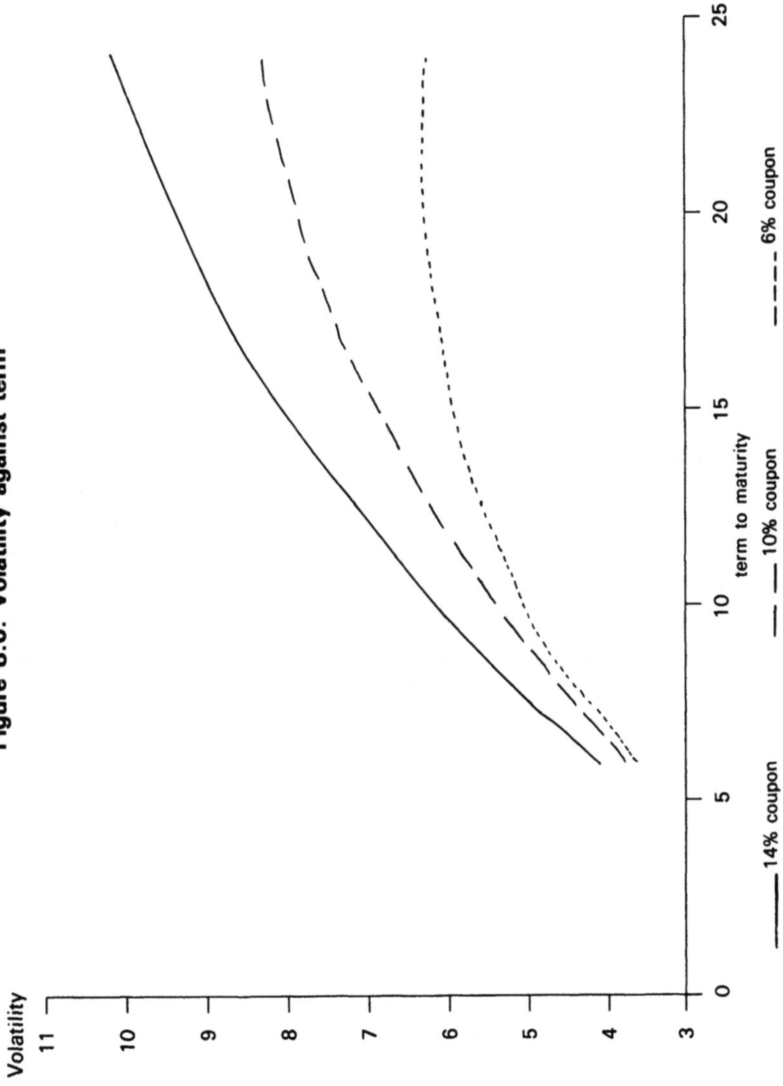

and demand of stock at particular maturities can then influence yields at that maturity and lead to a change in the shape of the yield curve. If, instead, expectations of future short rates dominate the determination of the yield curve, such influences would only be capable of changing the term structure to the extent that they influenced interest rate expectations (say, through the impact of funding on monetary growth and hence inflation).

The authorities' funding techniques

If the market is segmented in this way, then the maturity composition of the authorities' sales of new gilts can have an important influence on the shape of the yield curve. Specifically, an imbalance between the authorities' supply of new stock and demand within a given maturity band will influence yields in that band.

Recent experience with the authorities' funding techniques is interesting in this respect. From 1981 to 1985 the authorities refrained from making issues of new long dated stock. There were two main reasons for doing this. First they thought that by leaving the long end of the fixed interest market free of new issues of government stock, pressure on gilt yields would be moderated. It was hoped that this would stimulate renewed interest in the issue of bonds by the corporate sector and in turn, this would reduce the amount of intermediation performed by the banking system, thus leading to lower growth of broad money. Second, yields at the long end were thought to be too high in relation to official expectations of long run trends in inflation and, hence, interest rates. In the Autumn of 1981, for example, with the government committed to the reduction of inflation, it was difficult to justify long term funding at yields in excess of 16% per annum.

A change in funding techniques occurred at the end of 1981 when the authorities ceased making new issues of long dated stock. After the issue of Exchequer 15% 1997 in October 1981, no more new issues of long dated stock were made until that of Exchequer 10½% 2005 in January 1985. Although further tranches of existing stock were sold during the period, the maturity composition of new issues of gilts changed markedly (Table 8.2) — this brought about a change in the shape of the yield curve. In Figure 8.7, for example, we show yield curves on 1st October 1981 and 1st October 1984. The fall in long dated gilt yields relative to medium dated yields appeared to be closely correlated with changes in the relative amounts of long and medium dated gilts issued by the government (Figure 8.8).

Table 8.2: Maturity composition of gross official sales of gilts

£m; percentages of total gross sales in italic

Financial Years:	Total	Over 1 and up to 5 years	Over 5 and up to 15 years	Over 15 years and undated
1976/77	8395	2600 *(31)*	817 *(10)*	4978 *(59)*
1977/78	9615	2931 *(30)*	2826 *(29)*	3858 *(40)*
1978/79	7956	2192 *(28)*	1441 *(18)*	4323 *(54)*
1979/80	12634	2659 *(21)*	2969 *(24)*	7006 *(55)*
1980/81	15673	3030 *(19)*	6831 *(44)*	5812 *(37)*
1981/82	10636	3285 *(31)*	4254 *(40)*	3097 *(29)*
1982/83	10503	3841 *(37)*	5028 *(48)*	1634 *(16)*
1983/84	15363	6528 *(42)*	6206 *(40)*	2629 *(17)*
1984/85	15257	4900 *(32)*	6314 *(41)*	4043 *(26)*

Source: *BEQB*, Table 8.

It is too early to say decisively whether the new issue in 1985 represented a fundamental change in the authorities' attitude to funding at the long end. There remain, however, two key reasons why the authorities might desire to have a generally longer average maturity of government debt. First, longer dated debt is less liquid and therefore less likely to have an impact on spending in the economy: clearly, the shorter dated a government stock, the more 'money like' it becomes. Second, the amount of existing government bonds maturing on average each year is reduced: thus the problems of refinancing maturing debt are correspondingly eased.

Appendix: Models of gilt yields

In this section we consider in more detail three models of the determination of long term gilt yields. They are: a rational expectations model, and the long term gilt yield equations contained in the macroeconomic models of the Treasury and the Bank of England.

A rational expectations model [7]

In a world of *certainty and perfect foresight*, the total return from holding a long gilt will equal the return from holding a succession of short dated

Figure 8.7: Yield curves, October 1981 and October 1984

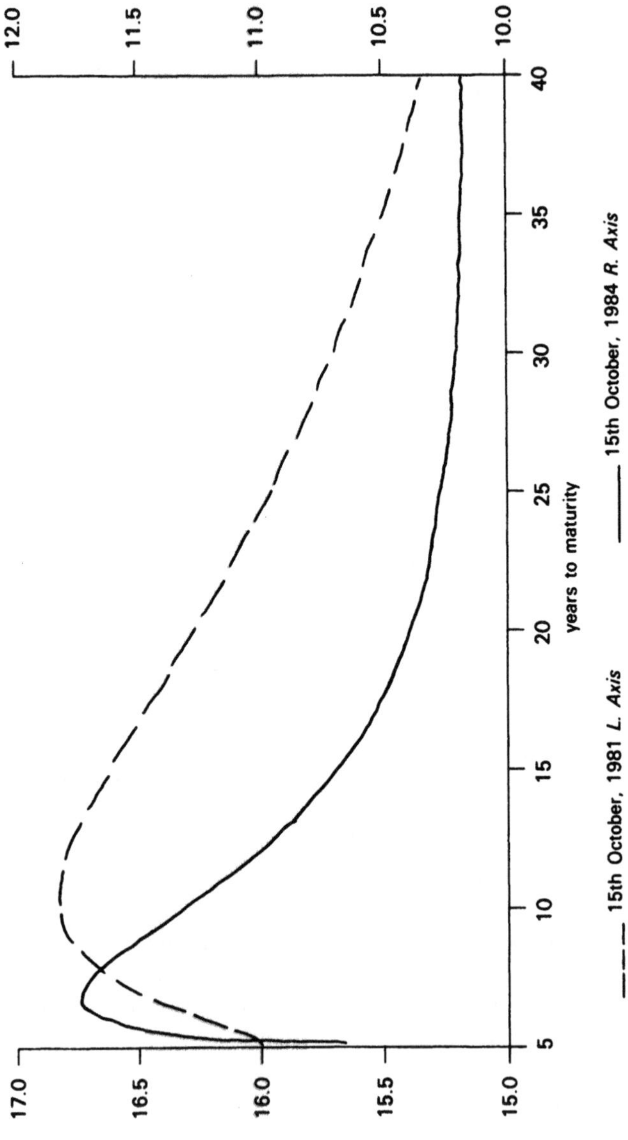

Figure 8.8: Funding policy and relative yields

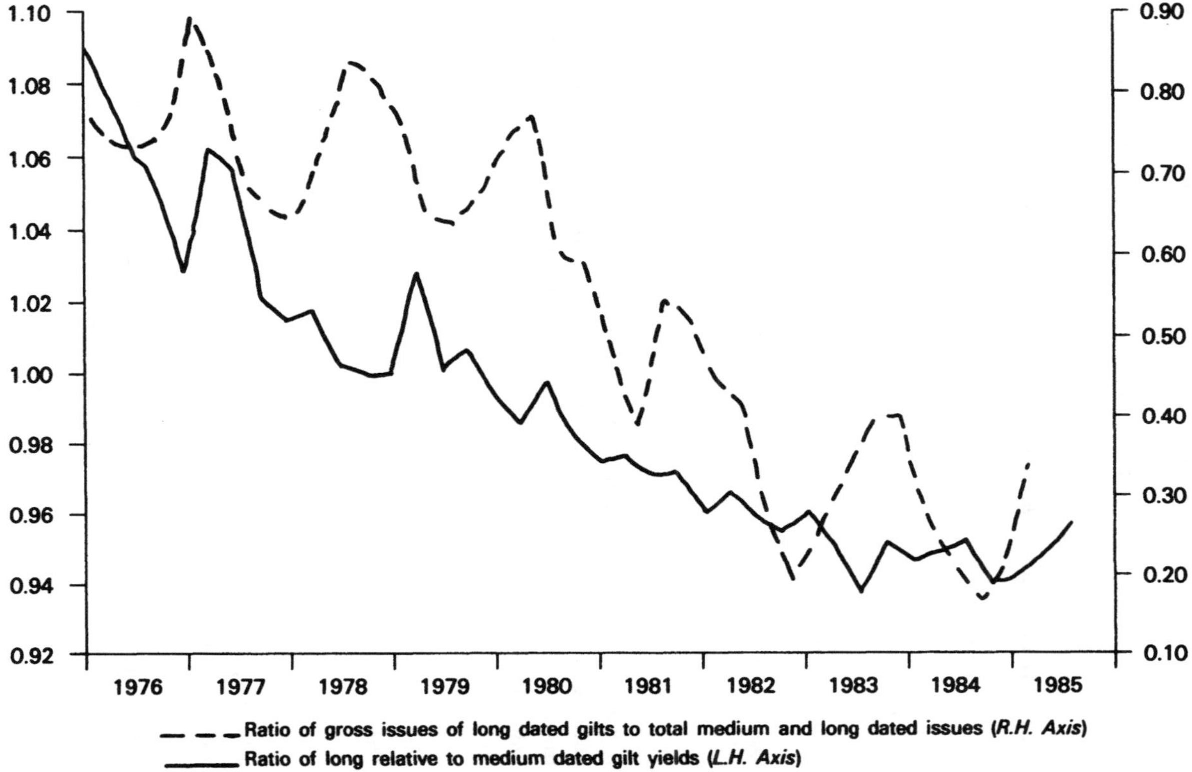

instruments. For simplicity, assume that the bond does not have a coupon (so the problem of the rate at which the coupons are reinvested is avoided) so that the total return from holding an N year bond up to maturity is $(1+R_t^N)^N$ where R is the annual return and t denotes that this is the return available at the time period t (assumed to be the 'base' period). Take, as the alternative investment a one year deposit giving returns of r_t in the first year, r_{t+1} in the second year and so on up to r_{t+N-1} in the final year.

Equality of returns over the N year period means that:

$$(1+R_t^N)^N = (1+r_t)\,(1+r_{t+1})\,\ldots\,(1+r_{t+N-1}) \tag{1a}$$

$$N\log(1+R_t^N) = \log(1+r_t) + \log(1+r_{t+1}) + \ldots + \log(1+r_{t+N-1}) \tag{1b}$$

Assuming for simplicity, that:

$\log(1+r) = r$ (which is broadly true over the likely range of values for r)

$$R_t^N = \frac{1}{N}\,(r_t + r_{t+1} + \ldots + r_{t+N-1}) \tag{2}$$

If we relax the assumption that investors have *perfect foresight* and assume instead that they form rational expectations of short rates beyond the current period, then we can replace the future short term interest rates with expected short rates in equation (2):

$$R_t^N = \frac{1}{N}\,(r_t + r_t{}^e{}_{+1} + \ldots + r_t{}^e{}_{+N-1}) \tag{3}$$

The expectations are defined as rational if:

$$r_t^e = r_t + U_t$$

where U_t is an error term with the properties that its mean value is zero and variance constant.

If the assumption of *certainty* is also relaxed, then a *risk premium* (K_t^N) can be introduced into equation (3) to give:

$$R_t^N = \frac{1}{N}\,(r_t + r_t{}^e{}_{+1} + \ldots + r_t{}^e{}_{+N-1}) + K_t^N \tag{4}$$

(This premium may reflect a number of factors discussed in detail later).

If we then decompose the short term rate r_t into its inflation component over the period (P_t) and the real interest rate (i_t), then:

$$r_t = i_t + P_t \tag{5}$$

Let i_t and P_t follow simple autoregressive processes of the following nature:

$$i_t = a_1 i_{t-1} + a_2 i_{t-2} + V_{i,t} \tag{6}$$

$$P_t = b_1 P_{t-1} + b_2 P_{t-2} + V_{p,t} \tag{7}$$

If the error terms ($V_{i,t}$ and $V_{p,t}$) are normally independently distributed, then (from (6)):

$$i_t^e = a_1 i_{t-1} + a_2 i_{t-2} \tag{6a}$$

and

$$P_t^e = b_1 P_{t-1} + b_2 P_{t-2} \tag{7a}$$

Equation (6) may now be used to form estimates of future expected real interest rates. From (6), it follows that:

$$i_{t+1} = a_1 i_t + a_2 i_{t-1} + V_{i,t+1}$$

and, under the same assumptions about the error term,

$$i_{t+1}^e = a_1(i_t^e) + a_2(i_{t-1})$$

$$= a_1(a_{1\,t-1} + a_{2\,t-2}) + a_2(i_{t-1})$$

$$= (a_1^2 + a_2) i_{t-1} + a_2 i_{t-2}$$

In turn, this can be used to forecast i_{t+2}^e and so on.

Each expected future real interest rate can be expressed in terms of i_{t-1} and i_{t-2}. Similarly, each expected future inflation rate can be expressed in terms of P_{t-1} and P_{t-2}.

Since the nominal interest rate r_t, is simply the sum of i_t and P_t, it follows that each expected future value of r_t can be expressed in terms of only i_{t-1}, i_{t-2}, P_{t-1} and P_{t-2}. Thus, returning to equation (4), we can express the return on the long bond as:

$$R_t^N = c_1 r_{t-1} + c_2 r_{t-2} + c_3 P_{t-1} + c_4 P_{t-2} + K_t^N + u_t$$

where $u_t^e = 0$.

The return on the long bond can thus be explained by past values of short term interest rates and inflationary expectations, and a constant term reflecting a risk premium. The risk premium term could encompass any number of factors including volatility and hedging influences. These would obviously vary depending on the maturity of the bond.

HM Treasury Macroeconomic Model (1982 version) [8]

The equation for the long term interest rate (RLONG) in the Treasury's macro-economic model is:

$$\text{RLONG} = 0.789 + 0.831 \text{ lg RLONG} + 0.311 \text{ RTB} - 0.252 \text{ g RTB} + 0.0552 \text{ PEXPF}$$

where:

RTB = Treasury bill rate
PEXPF = expected price inflation
g is a lag operator: g^i means that the variable is lagged by i quarters.

All data are quarterly.

The equation is similar to that resulting from the rational expectations model in that it contains short term interest rates and expected inflation. The constant term may be viewed as analogous to K_t^N in the rational expectations equation. However, the lag structure of the terms in the equation is rather different.

A one percentage point rise in the short term interest rate leads to a 0.311% point rise in long term rates in the same quarter; in the next quarter, the long term interest rate rises by a further 0.006% point, leading to a total rise of 0.317% point.

Expected price inflation in the Treasury model is, in turn, determined by the trend growth in wage costs, the rise in the unit value index for imports of all goods other than food, drink and tobacco, the growth of £M3 and the trend change in productivity.

Bank of England [9]

The Bank's equation for the long term interest rate — the gross redemption yield on twenty year gilts — is similar in that it contains a constant term, a short term interest rate and a variable measuring inflation expectations. These are augmented by a term measuring the ratio of the PSBR to nominal GDP, presumably reflecting a 'weight of funding' argument. Again, data are quarterly:

$$\text{RUKG} = 5.36 + 0.21\ \text{PEXP} + 0.19\ \text{D75A(-4)} \sum_{i=0}^{3} \text{Ai[100 PSBR/GDP£]-i-1}$$
$$+ 0.15(1\text{-D75A(-4)}) \sum_{i=0}^{3} \text{Ai[100 PSBR/GDP£]-i-2} + 0.28\ \text{RLA}$$

where: RUKG = gross redemption yield on twenty year gilts
PEXP = expected price inflation
PSBR/GDP£ = PSBR/GDP ratio
D75A = a dummy coefficient on the PSBR/GDP term allowing its influence on RUKG to be different before and after 1975.
RLA = local authority three month rate.

As there are no lagged effects, both the short and long run responses of the long rate to a rise in the short rate are identical. The magnitude of the effect is smaller than in the Treasury model: long rates rise by 0.28 of the rise in short rates. The influence of a change in inflation expectations on long rates is, however, around four times as large as in the Treasury model. Inflation expectations are generated in a simpler manner, being dependent on the expected change in the sterling/dollar exchange rate and the growth of producer output prices.

Notes and References

1. Bank of England, 'The future structure of the gilt edged market', *BEQB*, June 1985, pp.250-282.

2. A. L. Coleby, 'The Bank's operational procedures for meeting monetary objectives', *BEQB*, June 1983, pp.209-215.

3. The National Debt Commissioners are commissioners of the National Debt Office (NDO). The NDO was combined with the Public Works Loan

Board (PWLB, which lends central government funds to local authorities) in 1980 to form the National Investment and Loans Office (NILO). The seven National Debt Commissioners are:

1. The Governor of the Bank of England
2. The Deputy Governor of the Bank of England
3. The Chancellor of the Exchequer
4. The Speaker of the House of Commons
5. The Master of the Rolls
6. The Accountant General of the Supreme Court
7. The Lord Chief Justice.

Their main function is managing and investing the funds of a number of public sector bodies. The main ones are the National Insurance Fund and the National Savings Bank (until recently the funds of the Trustee Savings Bank were also managed). The funds of a number of other smaller bodies are also administered (among these are the Court Funds Investment Account, Insolvency Services Investment Account, the Redundancy Fund, The Maternity Pay Fund, the Crown Estate, and the National Heritage Fund). Money is deposited with the NDO and managed by it for these funds in accordance with agreed policy.

The National Debt Reduction Fund is also managed by the NDO. As well as using donations and bequests to reduce the outstanding amount of the National Debt, the fund is also responsible for managing the gilts which have sinking funds attached to them. One such stock is 3½% Conversion (undated), a certain proportion of which has to be bought in each half year; 3% Redemption 1986/96 also has a sinking fund attached to it, but there is no specified proportion bought in during any given period.

The GB conducts the business of the NDO in the gilt market, carrying out any sales, purchases or switches of stock which the NDO wishes to undertake. Purchases of gilts on behalf of the Commissioners are often executed by reserving for them a certain proportion of any new issue of stock. Sales of gilts by the NDO are one of the ways in which the GB can obtain unofficial taps'.

4. Bank of England, op.cit., p.251.

5. Such an approach was used, for example, in R. Coghlan Interpreting the money supply', *The Banker*, (July 1981).

6. See the papers by C.A.E. Goodhart and D. Gowland in the *Bulletin of Economic Research,* 1977 and 1978.

7. The example follows closely that set out in D.K.H. Begg, *The Rational Expectations Revolution in Macroeconomics,* Philip Allan, 1982.

8. See H.M. Treasury, 'H.M. Treasury Macroeconomic Model Technical Manual', (December 1982).

9. See 'Bank of England Model of the UK Economy', *Bank of England Discussion Paper Number 5,* (September 1979).

9 Conclusion

The aim of Chapters 3-8 has been to give an up-to-date description of the way in which the monetary authorities in the UK analyse monetary developments and operate in the related financial markets (especially the gilt edged and money markets). The analysis of monetary developments and the operation and conduct of policy are, however, almost continuously under review. In this final chapter we attempt to draw attention to some of the more important continuing questions surrounding monetary policy in the UK.

(i) The distinction between broad and narrow money

The book has drawn a rather sharp distinction between the analysis of broad money (Chapter 3) and narrow money (Chapter 4). The dichotomy reflects recent official thinking which has stressed the different uses of, and messages contained in, the behaviour of the two. Why is this distinction made? At its most basic, the distinction represents the difference between money used predominantly for transactions purposes and money used predominantly as a store of liquid financial wealth. Thus M0, the authorities' currently targetted measure of narrow money, consists mainly of notes and coin in circulation with the public which are used only to a small extent as a means of saving. £M3 adds (to cash in circulation with the public) deposits with banks which are more likely to be used as a store of liquid financial wealth. The private sector liquidity (PSL) aggregates go further, adding, for example, deposits with building societies. The appropriateness of the distinction between broad and narrow money has been questioned (see Chapter 4). It is interesting to note in this respect that M2 — a specially devised measure of transactions balances — is now thought to be behaving more like a measure of broad money. It includes, for example, the interest bearing cheque accounts which have recently become very popular with the personal sector: with these accounts the cheque book provides the facility for making instant payments without notice of withdrawal (thus making them effectively identical to the traditional non-interest bearing sight deposits) but the rate of interest paid on such deposits is comparable to that on traditional time deposits (included only in broader measures such as £M3). The result is that M2 includes deposits which are likely to be mainly used for savings purposes even though the deposits can be used easily for making payments.

By taking M0 as the targetted measure of narrow money the authorities have chosen an aggregate which is as far away as possible from this blurring of boundaries between money used for transactions purposes and money used as a store of liquid financial wealth. M0 or, more strictly, just the (large) proportion of it which is notes and coin in circulation, has another key property. No attempt has been, or is likely to be, made to control the amount of cash in circulation from the supply side: the amount of cash in circulation is determined entirely by the banks' and public's demand for it. This means that, when estimating an equation for M0, one can be confident that one is identifying the demand for M0. The Treasury is confident in its ability to explain the behaviour of M0 by such an equation, using consumers' expenditure, interest rates and various technological factors (affecting the use of cash relative to other types of money) as the explanatory factors.

Attempts by the authorities to explain the behaviour of broad money in an analogous way have consistently failed during the 1970s and 1980s. In large part this is probably due to the fact that the demand for bank credit has been the dominant influence on the size of banks' balance sheets during the period. Banks have been able, using the technique of liability management, to bid for (wholesale) deposits in order to match this demand for credit.

(ii) Why the counterparts approach to £M3?

In this environment, the analysis of £M3 has centred not so much on the behaviour of the deposits included in the measurement of £M3 but rather on its credit counterparts. The way in which these are constructed is relatively straightforward: the balance sheet of the UK monetary sector can be viewed as consisting of £M3 deposits plus other liabilities of the monetary sector on one side which must equal total assets on the other side. £M3 can thus be viewed as the simple difference between total assets and non-£M3 liabilities. Expressing the monetary sector's balance sheet in this way and then expressing the public sector's demand for credit from the UK monetary sector as the residual of of its borrowing requirement and other sources of finance gives the familiar counterparts to £M3 identity. £M3 is expressed (simplifying a little) as the PSBR minus sales of government debt to the non-bank private sector plus the private sector's demand for credit from the banks plus external flows affecting money and the change in various non-deposit liabilities. (The development of the £M3 counterparts is discussed in detail in Chapter 3). Although the counterparts identity is just a statistical artefact based on these identities, it has come to be of central importance in the analysis and presentation of policy. It provides a framework within which fiscal policy (reflected in the size of the PSBR), the extent to which government borrowing is financed outside the monetary sector (i.e. funding policy), the expansion of the private sector's demand for credit and the influence of external flows (including official intervention) can be brought together in one summary statistic.

The counterparts approach, coming as it does from expressing a subset of banks' liabilities as equal to their total assets minus the remaining liabilities, can be used for any measure of money. If the rationale for the counterparts approach is that banks' balance sheet size is determined predominantly by the demand for credit, with the banks bidding for deposits in order to match this, it would appear logical to use the counterparts approach for measures of money which are predominantly influenced by bank liability management. That points towards the use of a broad aggregate such as £M3 (which includes large time deposits and CDs, key instruments of liability management) and away from an aggregate like nibM1 (the deposits included in which are unlikely to be responsive to such a technique).

(iii) Problems with £M3

One of the main problems with £M3 during the period in which it has been at the centre of monetary policy has been the difficulty of controlling the growth of bank lending to the private sector. The demand for bank credit does not appear to be particularly sensitive (at least in the short term) to changes in short term interest rates and for various reasons (discussed in Chapter 3), direct controls have been eschewed. In these circumstances, overfunding of the PSBR has become the main technique of short term control of £M3. This has led to large money market shortages (see Chapter 6) and possible distortion to the monetary statistics from round-tripping. Furthermore, the deposits included in £M3 have become more attractive as a home for liquid financial balances, further complicating the assessment of the behaviour of the aggregate. These difficulties have led to some downgrading of the relevance of £M3 by the authorities, who are now placing rather more emphasis on the behaviour of narrower measures of money (see Chapter 5).

(iv) Banks and building societies

Banks and building societies are becoming more similar in a number of respects. Building societies have recently adopted, albeit to a limited extent, the technique of liability management. The ability to issue CDs has, as with the banks, been of key importance in their ability to do this. Mortgage queues — one of the more visible effects of building society asset management — have now largely disappeared. The societies have introduced more attractive types of deposit for the personal sector: indeed, the types of deposit offered by the banks and the societies are becoming almost indistinguishable. In this environment, it seems more appropriate to concentrate on a broader aggregate such as PSL2 which includes both bank and building society deposits.

Furthermore, as the societies become more active liability managers it would seem sensible to analyse this aggregate in terms of its credit counterparts. Bank and building society lending to the non-bank private sector would then replace just bank lending as the main private sector credit counterpart. Borrowing from building societies is quite clearly an important source of finance for the personal sector and one which is not used exclusively for house purchase. Indeed, the practice of 'equity withdrawal' is well recognised: it is said to occur when net new loans for house purchase exceed net private sector expenditure on housing. The excess can be used for a variety of purposes — to repay other borrowing, to finance interest payments, to increase holdings of other assets or to sustain consumption.

Although it would thus seem logical to attach greater weight to a broader measure of liquidity such as PSL2, and its counterparts, the authorities have chosen to place less emphasis on that aggregate. PSL2 was demoted from a target aggregate in the 1982/3 and 1983/4 target periods, to an aggregate of special importance in monitoring trends in broad money in the 1984/5 target period, to having no special significance in the 1985/6 target period.

(v) The demise of liability management

At the same time as the building societies are becoming more orientated towards liability management, there are some signs that the banks may be starting to place more reliance once again on asset management. There are three main factors behind this change. First, intermediation by the banking sector is being undermined by the process of securitisation — bank customers go directly to the securities markets in order to meet their financing needs; second, lending policies have become more cautious in the face of international debt problems; and, third, bank failures and solvency crises (particularly in the USA) have underlined the problems associated with relying on a substantial wholesale deposit base.

There are even some tentative signs that building society mortgage business is being influenced by the process of securitisation. A secondary market in mortgages in the UK, similar to that which is well established in the USA, is clearly a possibility over the coming years. In such circumstances even broader aggregates such as PSL2 would fail accurately to record the extent of financial intermediation in the economy.

(vi) The usefulness of the quantity theory of money

All the talk of counterparts and liability management, appears a long way from the simple quantity theory of money (see Chapter 2). This states that the quantity of money in circulation (M) times its velocity of circulation (V) must be equal to nominal incomes in the economy (which, in turn, can be decomposed into price (P) and output (T) components). The quantity theory, as well as providing the theoretical underpinning of monetarist policies, proved in the early 1980s to be the basis of political rhetoric on monetary control: with the the growth of M fixed and an assumption of stability (if not constancy) in V, then high inflation would simply leave less room for real growth in the economy. The wayward behaviour of velocity, certainly in the early years of the 1980s, seriously undermined the basis of this presentation. With the banks free from direct constraints on the size of their balance sheets and the reintermediation of banking business following the abolition of the 'corset', £M3 grew strongly and its velocity fell in the early 1980s. It clearly did not bear a close relationship to the behaviour of nominal GDP. In large part this can be attributed to the removal of these constraints on banks' lending coupled with their ability to liability manage. Of course, it may be that after such structural changes the relationship of £M3 to nominal GDP returns to a more stable pattern. Indeed, a trend decline in the velocity of £M3 since 1981 is evident, with £M3 growing around 3.5% per annum faster than nominal GDP on average (see Figure 2.2).

As discussed above, narrow measures of money are less susceptible to such structural changes in the banking system. In the extreme case of notes and coin in circulation, for example, one can be sure that the demand for that measure is being identified by the series of data on the stock of cash in circulation. The Treasury appear confident in their ability to explain the behaviour of cash; and its velocity (unlike that of £M3) may be reasonably stable: in this case, its behaviour may give a reasonably reliable indication of the behaviour of money GDP.

(vii) Money GDP as an alternative

Of course, if one is using measures of money as just an indicator of the concurrent behavior of nominal income in the economy it may be more appropriate to examine the behaviour of nominal income itself. Such a proposal has been put forward by Sam Brittan (see Chapter 5). The standard objection to this is that the GDP statistics are only available after a considerable time lag and, moreover, are subject to substantial revision. The approach has been likened to driving the economy by looking in the reversing mirror. Of course, the underlying behaviour of nominal GDP can be assessed by examining the various monthly indicators on the real economy. In the USA, for example, although nominal GNP growth has come to take on greater significance in policy decisions, it is not just the behaviour of the GNP data itself which is assessed. A wide range of monthly indicators are useful in examining trends in nominal income and the time lag involved in the availability of the data is no longer than that for the monetary aggregates.

There remains the broader question of the need for intermediate financial targets as opposed to targets for some final objective (such as nominal GDP growth or inflation). In the form of a fixed exchange rate (in the period up until 1971) or in the form of targets for domestic monetary aggregates (announced since 1976) these have been a virtually constant feature of post-war UK economic policy. The brief period between the two regimes was one of considerable turmoil, in which acute overheating in the early 1970s led to severe inflationary problems. The surge in inflation was, of course, partly due to the substantial external shock of the sharp rise in oil prices, but developments in this period serve as a reminder of the risks of macroeconomic management in the absence of intermediate financial targets. The main requirement of an intermediate indicator is that it gives leading information about developments in final objectives. In the recent past the most important of these final objectives has been inflation, with money as the most important intermediate objective.

(viii) Money as a leading indicator of inflation

When monetary targets were first introduced in the UK, it was thought that broader measures of money gave more reliable information about future inflation than did the narrower measures, which appeared to be more closely related to current, rather than future, developments. The Treasury's recent work on this subject appears to have reversed that conclusion with the narrower aggregates now thought to give a better leading indication.

This does not, however, appear to sit comfortably with the view that narrow money is demand determined. One view of the link between money and inflation would, for example, see excess money growth (represented by observed money growth running ahead of demand) as leading to future inflation, as economic agents seek to reallocate such excess money balances. These excess money balances seem much more likely to be held in interest bearing deposits, not included in very narrow measures of money such as MO. In this sense it seems unlikely that narrow money should provide a leading indication of inflation. Of course, the transmission mechanism — the process whereby changes in the money supply lead through to future inflation — continues to be the source of some dispute (some of the channels are discussed in Chapter 3). The monetarists have always maintained that in view of the diversity of ways in which money flows impact on the economy, the question of the choice of monetary aggregate which provides the best leading indication of inflation should be an empirical one: as the recent UK experience demonstrates, however, such an analysis is not straightforward.

(ix) The exchange rate as a monetary indicator

If the link between money and future inflation is both analytically and empirically obscure, it may be more appropriate to place greater reliance on the behaviour of the exchange rate as an indicator of future inflation. Not only are variations in the exchange rate viewed as one of the main mechanisms through which monetary policy works, but also the empirical link between exchange rate changes and inflation appears to be reasonably well determined. Certainly, in mid-1985 the authorities do appear to have come to place greater reliance on this as a monetary indicator. The fall in the exchange rate at the end of 1984 and the start of 1985 led to a sharp rise in the cost of raw materials in the early months of 1985. The sharp rise in the exchange rate from the Spring of that year onwards was, equally, an important influence behind the fall in the cost of such materials later in the year. Variations in the exchange rate exert an important influence on the behaviour of inflation in other ways — the impact on corporate profitability and hence on the ability to meet wage demands, and the influence on the level of interest rates and hence mortgage rates and the RPI are two examples.

The inflationary consequences of exchange rate changes as well as the problems associated with exchange rate volatility itself have led to widespread calls for a return to the use of a fixed exchange rate — rather than a monetary target — as an intermediate objective of policy. In current circumstances, full membership of the European Monetary System (EMS) is one of the more obvious ways in which such an objective may be expressed. An alternative would be a target for the sterling exchange rate index.

Such proposals have been considered at regular intervals for some time. The authorities' objections to full membership of the EMS remain twofold: first, it would seriously constrain their ability to pursue independent monetary objectives and, second, with the UK heavily dependent on oil, changes in oil market conditions would have a different effect on sterling compared to the other currencies in the EMS block, threatening greater instability in the system. Furthermore, there is the problem of selecting the particular set of bilateral exchange rates at which to enter the system. There is no uniquely correct value of, say, the rate for sterling against the deutschmark. Calculations based on estimated real exchange rates can give some indication of the 'appropriate' rate but these calculations are, by their nature, imprecise.

There is no reason why targets for the exchange rate and monetary aggregates should be mutually exclusive. The authorities could, for example, tolerate a weakening of the exchange rate if the domestic monetary aggregates were on target; and tolerate above-target monetary growth if the exchange rate were strengthening. Indeed, as discussed in Chapter 5, the UK authorities appear recently to have been operating in this way, although no target band for the exchange rate has been made explicit.

Appendix 1: Official Interest Rates, 1932 to 1985[1]

Date of change		New rate (per cent)
1932	30 June	2
1939	24 August	4
	28 September	3
	26 October	2
1951	8 November	2½
1952	12 March	4
1953	17 September	3½
1954	13 May	3
1955	27 January	3½
	24 February	4½
1956	16 February	5½
1957	7 February	5
	19 September	7
1958	20 March	6
	22 May	5½
	19 June	5
	14 August	4½
	20 November	4
1960	21 January	5
	23 June	6

Date of change		New rate (per cent)
1960	27 October	5½
	8 December	5
1961	25 July	7
	5 October	6½
	2 November	6
1962	8 March	5½
	22 March	5
	26 April	4½
1963	3 January	4
1964	27 February	5
	23 November	7
1965	3 June	6
1966	14 July	7
1967	26 January	6½
	16 March	6
	4 May	5½
	19 October	6
	9 November	6½
	18 November	8
1968	21 March	7½
	19 September	7

Date of change		New rate (per cent)	
1969	27 February	8	
1970	5 March	$7\frac{1}{2}$	
	15 April	7	
1971	1 April	6	
	2 September	5	
1972	22 June	6	

Date of change		New rate (per cent)	
	13 October	$7\frac{1}{4}$	
	27 October	$7\frac{1}{2}$	
	1 December	$7\frac{3}{4}$	
	8 December	8	
	22 December	9	
1973	19 January	$8\frac{3}{4}$	
	23 March	$8\frac{1}{2}$	
	13 April	8	
	19 April	$8\frac{1}{4}$	
	11 May	8	
	18 May	$7\frac{3}{4}$	
	22 June	$7\frac{1}{2}$	
	20 July	9	
	27 July	$11\frac{1}{2}$	
	19 October	$11\frac{1}{4}$	
	13 November	13	*
1974	4 January	$12\frac{3}{4}$	
	1 February	$12\frac{1}{2}$	
	5 April	$12\frac{1}{4}$	
	11 April	12	
	24 May	$11\frac{3}{4}$	
	20 September	$11\frac{1}{2}$	
1975	17 January	$11\frac{1}{4}$	
	24 January	11	
1975	7 February	$10\frac{3}{4}$	
	14 February	$10\frac{1}{2}$	
	7 March	$10\frac{1}{4}$	
	21 March	10	
	18 April	$9\frac{3}{4}$	
	2 May	10	
	25 July	11	
	3 October	12	
	14 November	$11\frac{3}{4}$	
	28 November	$11\frac{1}{2}$	
	24 December	$11\frac{1}{4}$	
1976	2 January	11	
	16 January	$10\frac{3}{4}$	
	23 January	$10\frac{1}{2}$	
	30 January	10	
	6 February	$9\frac{1}{2}$	
	27 February	$9\frac{1}{4}$	
	5 March	9	
	23 April	$10\frac{1}{2}$	
	21 May	$11\frac{1}{2}$	
	10 September	13	
	7 October	15	*
	19 November	$14\frac{3}{4}$	
	17 December	$14\frac{1}{2}$	
	24 December	$14\frac{1}{4}$	
1977	7 January	14	
	21 January	$13\frac{1}{4}$	
	28 January	$12\frac{1}{4}$	
	3 February	12	*
	10 March	11	
	18 March	$10\frac{1}{2}$	
	31 March	$9\frac{1}{2}$	
	7 April	$9\frac{1}{4}$	
	15 April	9	
	22 April	$8\frac{3}{4}$	
	29 April	$8\frac{1}{4}$	

Date of change	New rate (per cent)	
1977 13 May	8	
5 August	$7\frac{1}{2}$	
12 August	7	
9 September	$6\frac{1}{2}$	
16 September	6	
7 October	$5\frac{1}{2}$	
14 October	5	
25 November	7	
1978 6 January	$6\frac{1}{2}$	
11 April	$7\frac{1}{2}$	*
5 May	$8\frac{3}{4}$	*
12 May	9	*
8 June	10	*
9 November	$12\frac{1}{2}$	*
1979 8 February	14	*
1 March	13	*
5 April	12	*
12 June	14	*
15 November	17	*
1980 3 July	16	*
24 November	14	*
1981 10 March	12	*

Date of change	New rate (per cent)
4 September[2]	$12\frac{11}{16}$
15 September	$13\frac{15}{16}-14\frac{1}{16}$
18 September	$14\frac{1}{16}-\frac{1}{8}$
23 September	$14\frac{1}{4}-\frac{3}{8}$
25 September	$14\frac{1}{2}$
30 September	$14\frac{3}{4}-15\frac{1}{2}$
1 October	$15-15\frac{3}{4}$
9 November	$14\frac{5}{8}-\frac{3}{4}$
25 November	$14\frac{9}{16}$
4 December	$14\frac{3}{8}$

Date of change	New rate (per cent)
1982 18 January	$14\frac{15}{16}$
19 January	$14\frac{1}{4}$
20 January	$14\frac{1}{8}$
21 January	14
22 January	$13\frac{7}{8}$
22 February	$13\frac{13}{16}$
25 February	$13\frac{5}{8}$
10 March	$13\frac{1}{4}$
16 April	$13\frac{1}{8}$
8 June	$12\frac{5}{8}$
8 July	$12\frac{1}{2}-\frac{9}{16}$
12 July	$12\frac{1}{4}-\frac{3}{8}$
13 July	$12\frac{1}{8}$
26 July	$11\frac{15}{16}-12$
28 July	$11\frac{13}{16}-\frac{7}{8}$
29 July	$11\frac{3}{4}$
30 July	$11\frac{5}{8}$
2 August	$11\frac{9}{16}$
4 August	$11\frac{1}{2}$
16 August	$11\frac{3}{8}-\frac{7}{16}$
17 August	$11\frac{1}{4}-\frac{5}{16}$
18 August	$11\frac{1}{4}$
23 August	11
26 August	$10\frac{7}{8}$
27 August	$10\frac{5}{8}-\frac{3}{4}$
31 August	$10\frac{5}{8}$
27 September	$10\frac{1}{2}-\frac{5}{8}$
28 September	$10\frac{3}{8}-\frac{1}{2}$
29 September	$10\frac{1}{4}$
30 September	$10\frac{1}{8}$
12 October	$9\frac{5}{8}-\frac{3}{4}$
13 October	$9\frac{5}{8}$
1 November	$9\frac{3}{8}-\frac{5}{8}$
2 November	$9\frac{1}{8}$
26 November	$10-10\frac{1}{8}$
29 November	10
1983 12 January	11

Date of change	New rate (per cent)	Date of change	New rate (per cent)
1983 15 March	$10\frac{9}{16}$	1984 9 August	11
13 April	$10\frac{5}{16}$-$\frac{1}{2}$	16 August	$10\frac{3}{4}$
14 April	$10\frac{1}{16}$-$\frac{1}{4}$	17 August	$10\frac{1}{2}$
15 April	$10\frac{1}{16}$	5 November	10
13 June	$9\frac{13}{16}$-$\frac{15}{16}$	19 November	$9\frac{3}{4}$
14 June	$9\frac{9}{16}$	23 November	$9\frac{1}{2}$
3 October	$9\frac{1}{16}$		
1984 7 March	$8\frac{13}{16}$	1985 14 January[3]	$11\frac{7}{8}$-12
14 March	$8\frac{9}{16}$	28 January	$13\frac{7}{8}$
10 May	$9\frac{1}{16}$	20 March	$13\frac{3}{8}$
29 June	$8\frac{7}{8}$	28 March	$12\frac{7}{8}$
6 July	10	19 April	$12\frac{3}{8}$
11 July	12	12 July	$11\frac{7}{8}$
8 August	$11\frac{1}{2}$	26 July	$11\frac{3}{8}$

Notes:

1. The official interest rate is defined as:
   Bank Rate (from 30 June 1932 to 12 October 1972).
   Bank of England's minimum lending rate to the market (from 13 October 1972 to 19 August 1981).
   Bank of England's Dealing Rate for Band 1 bank bills (from 20 August 1981 onwards).

2. The first time, under the new arrangements, that the Bank bought band 1 bills outright. There had been no significant move in market interest rates between 20 August (when MLR ceased to be posted continuously) and that date.

3. MLR was reintroduced at the rate of 12% for one day only.

* Indicates that MLR was administered, not determined by formula.

Appendix 2: Monetary Policy Measures, 1970 to 1985

(Changes in official interest rates are listed separately in Appendix 1)

1970

April	LCBs were asked to limit the increase in sterling lending to the private sector and overseas to 5% over the twelve months to March 1971. Other banks were allowed 7% growth. Within the guidelines, lending should be directed to exporters; there should be no increase in lending for personal consumption. A further call for special deposits was made raising their level to 2½% of eligible liabilities for the LCBs and 1¼% for the SCBs.
July	Banks were requested to reduce the rate of growth of lending, which was growing faster than that consistent with the April guidance.
October	A further call for special deposits was made raising their level to 3½% of eligible liabilities for LCBs and 1¾% for SCBs.

1971

January	Foreign currency borrowing to finance domestic expenditure was to be for a term of at least five years.
March	Quantitative credit controls were eased. It was requested that lending in restricted categories should not rise beyond 107½% of the March 1970 level for clearing banks, and 109½% for other banks, in the second quarter of 1971.

May	Competition and Credit Control' (CCC), a consultative document, was published. It was suggested that the authorities would place less emphasis on direct control of lending to the private sector. Instead, the intention was to place greater emphasis on variations in interest rates to influence the demand for credit. These were to be backed up, if needed, by calls for special deposits.
June	It was requested that, pending the introduction of the new credit control arrangements, lending by clearing banks should not exceed 110% of March 1970 levels by mid-September. The limit for other banks was 112%.
July	Hire purchase controls were removed.
August	Measures taken to discourage inflow of capital from abroad, including restrictions on the payment of interest on new non-resident sterling balances.
September	New credit control arrangements, broadly along the lines of CCC, became effective from mid-September. Reserve assets ratio introduced.
December	Measures taken to restrict foreign capital inflows were removed.

1972

June	Sterling was floated.
August	Banks were asked to ensure that finance was available to sustain industrial expansion. If necessary, this should be at the expense of finance to property companies.
October	Bank Rate replaced by Minimum Lending Rate (MLR). This was determined by formula: it was to be ½% above the average rate of discount for Treasury bills at the most recent tender, rounded to the nearest ¼% above. The Bank reserved the right to suspend the formula.

November Special deposits called from banks and finance houses equal to 1% of eligible liabilities.

December A further call for special deposits, making a total of 3% of eligible liabilities.

1973

July A further call for special deposits, making a total of 4% of eligible liabilities.

September Banks asked to restrict personal credit, to restrict further lending on property and financial transactions and to discourage interest arbitrage activities. Banks asked to limit interest paid on deposits of less than £10,000 to 9½% to protect building society inflows.

October Minimum term for foreign currency borrowing to finance domestic expenditure reduced to two years (from five years).

November Further call for special deposits, making 6% of eligible liabilities.

December Supplementary Special Deposits scheme (SSD, or 'corset') introduced. Banks were required to place supplementary special deposits with the Bank of England if their interest bearing eligible liabilities (IBELs) grew faster than a specified rate (8% for the first six months).
Hire purchase controls reintroduced.
The balance of the November special deposits call (½% on 27th December and ½% on 2nd January) was revoked. This left special deposits at 5% of eligible liabilities.

1974

January Special deposits reduced to 4½% of eligible liabilities.

April Special deposits reduced to 3%. The SSD scheme was to be continued for a further six months, with IBELs allowed to grow by 1½% per month.

November — SSD extended for a further six months, with the allowed growth again 1½% per month.
Banks and finance houses asked to maintain restraint on lending to persons, to property companies and for purely financial transactions.

1975

February — SSD scheme suspended.
Guidance on lending was maintained.
Request to banks not to pay more than 9½% on deposits under £10,000 was withdrawn.

December — D. Healey, Chancellor of the Exchequer, announced that Domestic Credit Expansion (DCE) should be £9bn in 1976/77.

1976

January — Special deposits reduced to 2%.

February — Special deposits raised to 3%.

April — (6th, Budget) D. Healey, Chancellor of the Exchequer, announced that, after two years in which M3 had grown more slowly than GDP, he would expect their growth rates to come into line in the 1976/77 financial year.

July — Healey announced that for the financial year 1976/77 as a whole, money supply (M3) growth should amount to around 12%.

September — Special deposits to be raised to 4%.

October — Special deposits to be raised to 6%.

November — SSD scheme reintroduced. Base was the average level of IBELs on August, September and October make-up days. Rate of growth 3% for first six months and ½% per month for further two months. Penalties were to be: for growth of IBELs 3% or less above limit, 5% of excess to be placed in

	SSDs; growth 3-5% above limit, 25% of excess to be placed in SSDs; 5% and above, 50% to be placed in SSDs.
December	The UK borrowed from the IMF and sent a 'Letter of Intent' in which the authorities agreed to limits on DCE of £9bn in 1976/77; £7.7bn in 1977/78 and £6bn in 1978/79. £M3 growth of 9-13% in 1976/77 was thought to be compatible with the DCE limit.

1977

January	Special deposits reduced to 2%.
March	Special deposits raised to 3%.
May	SSD scheme continued for a further six months. Base was the average level of IBELs on the April to June make-up days. Growth of ½% per month to be allowed.
August	SSD scheme suspended. Growth of DCE and £M3 both within target.
October	Official intervention to 'cap' sterling was withdrawn and the currency strengthened substantially.

1978

April	(11th, Budget) £M3 target range 8-12% for 1978/79. Targets to be rebased once every six months.
May	MLR formula terminated. In future, MLR to be determined by administrative decision.
June	SSD scheme re-activated. Base period six months from November 1977/April 1978, permitted growth 4% to August/October 1978. Same penalty rates as with November 1978 scheme. Special deposits reduced to 1½%.
July	Special deposits raised to 2%.

August	SSD scheme continued for a further eight months. Base period September/November 1978; allowable growth 1% per month.
September	Special deposits raised to 3%.
November	Growth of £M3 below 8-12% target range in six months April-October 1978. Target range for six months October-April remained 8-12%.

1979

February	Special deposits reduced from 3% to 1% because of pressure on reserve assets; to be restored to 2% on 9th March and 3% on 30th March.
March	1% recall of special deposits due on 9th March suspended. 1% recall on 30th March delayed to 8th May. In addition, special deposits were reduced to zero between 19th and 30th March. A 1% recall on 23rd April was announced to take the level to 2%, then to 3% with the 8th May recall.
April	SSD scheme continued for a further three months. Penalty free growth 1% per month.
June	(12th, First Conservative Budget) Announcement of relaxation of exchange controls. SSD scheme continued for a further three months. Penalty free growth again 1% per month. £M3 target range 7-11% from mid-June 1979.
July	Temporary reduction of special deposits to ½%. Recalls of ½% on 3rd August and 1% on 13th August to return rate to 2%. Recall of ½% on 3rd August subsequently delayed to 10th September.
September	(23rd) Announcement that all remaining exchange controls will be removed with effect from 24th October.
November	SSD scheme continued for a further six months. Penalty free growth again 1% per month. £M3 growth of 2% in October, took annualised growth since

mid-June to 14%, above the 7-11% range. Target range was extended for a further six months (i.e. to mid-October 1980).

1980

January — Temporary reduction in special deposits from 2% to zero, effective from 16th January. Restoration to 1% on 8th February and 2% on 7th March.

February — Special deposits recall due on 8th February delayed to 8th April; that for 7th March delayed to 14th May.

March — Monetary Control Green Paper published.
(26th, Budget) MTFS announced, with a progressive reduction in money supply growth. Target range for £M3 to be 7-11% in 1980/81 with the target period defined as the fourteen months mid-February 1980 to mid-April 1981. Progressive reduction in £M3 growth with target ranges declining by 1% in each of the subsequent years to 4-8% in 1983/84. SSD scheme to be discontinued after mid-June.

April — Special deposits call due on 8th April delayed to 16th June.

May — Cancellation of 1% special deposits recall due on 14th May.

June — Cancellation of 1% special deposits recall due on 16th June.

September — Publication of Bank of England papers on 'The Measurement of Liquidity' and 'The Measurement of Capital'.

November — Publication of a background note 'Methods of Monetary Control' following from discussions in response to the March 'Green Paper'. Reserve assets ratio to be abolished. Future of cash ratio to be considered. Bank to discuss with the banks collection of data on retail deposits. Three changes to be made to Bank's intervention in the money market: (i) intervention will place a greater emphasis on dealing in bills rather than 'discount window' lending; (ii) aim will be 'to keep very short term interest rates within an unpublished band'. The Bank might cease to announce MLR; (iii) 'the Bank's operations would be broadly intended to offset daily cash flows between the Bank and the money markets'. Technique of deliberately over-issuing Treasury bills to be abandoned.

1981

January The minimum reserve assets ratio was reduced from 12½% to 10% of eligible liabilities.

March (10th, Budget) New target range for £M3 6-10% for 14 months mid-February 1981 to mid-April 1982. Reserve assets ratio to be phased out. Introduction of index-linked gilts available to pension funds, life insurance companies and friendly societies.

(12th) Publication by the Bank of 'Monetary Control: next steps', following on from the background paper 'Methods of Monetary Control' published in November 1980. Requirement for the LCBs to hold 1½% of their eligible liabilities in deposits at the Bank to be replaced by the requirement for all recognised banks and licensed deposit taking institutions to hold non-operational non-interest bearing deposits with the Bank. The LCBs will maintain, as well as these deposits, 'such balances as are necessary for clearing purposes'. Bank had placed greater reliance on dealing in bills rather than discount window lending since November 1980. Bank to extend list of banks whose bills are eligible for rediscount at the Bank.

August (5th) Publication by the Bank of 'Monetary Control Provisions' following on from 'Monetary Control: next steps'. Level of non-operational non-interest bearing deposits to be set at ½% of eligible liabilities. Level to be changed each six months in relation to average eligible liabilities in previous six months. Special deposits scheme retained, applying to all institutions with eligible liabilities of £10m or more. New, extended, list of 'eligible banks' (i.e. those banks whose bills are eligible for rediscount at the Bank) published. Eligible banks required to keep specified ratios of secured money with the discount houses and/or secured call money with money brokers and gilt edged jobbers.

	(20th) New arrangements for monetary control take effect. MLR suspended. Minimum reserve assets ratio abolished.

1982

March	(9th, Budget) Target range of 8-12% set for M1, £M3 and PSL2. Target period 14 months mid-February 1982 to mid-April 1983.

1983

March	(15th, Budget) Target range of 7-11% set for M1, £M3 and PSL2. Target period 14 months mid-February 1982 to mid-April 1983.
October	Nigel Lawson, new Chancellor of the Exchequer (after the re-election of the Conservative government in June) in his speech at the Mansion House discusses his review of monetary policy. Narrower measures of money linked more closely to future inflation.

1984

March	(13th, Budget) Target ranges set for M0 of 4-8% and £M3 of 6-10%. Target period 14 months mid-February 1984 to mid-April 1985.

1985

January	(14th) MLR re-introduced, at the rate of 12%, for one day only.
March	(19th, Budget) Target ranges set for M0 of 3-7% and £M3 of 5-9%.
May	Announcement in the Treasury's 'Economic Progress Report' that target ranges for monetary growth are to relate to the twelve month growth rate, rather than the annualised rate of growth since the start of the target period. Target periods are now to be for financial years.

Index

MIX
Papier aus verantwortungsvollen Quellen
Paper from responsible sources
FSC® C105338

If you have any concerns about our products,
you can contact us on
ProductSafety@springernature.com

In case Publisher is established outside the EU,
the EU authorized representative is:
Springer Nature Customer Service Center GmbH
Europaplatz 3, 69115 Heidelberg, Germany

Printed by Libri Plureos GmbH
in Hamburg, Germany